STUDY GUIDE

INDIANA CHRISTIAN UNIVERSITY

DEMONOLOGY
&
DELIVERANCE

VOLUME II

By
DR. LESTER SUMRALL

530 E. IRELAND ROAD
SOUTH BEND, INDIANA 46614
U.S.A.

This special study guide is a college workbook. The space provided for your personal notes is for the text to grow into your own material.

Videotapes and audiotapes are available to assist you.

All scriptures, unless otherwise noted, are taken from the *King James Version* of the Bible.

All scriptures marked NKJV are taken from the *New King James Version* of the Bible. Copyright 1982 by Thomas Nelson, Inc., Nashville, TN.

DEMONOLOGY & DELIVERANCE II
ISBN No. 0-937580-64-3
Copyright © by Lester Sumrall Evangelistic Association

Printed by SUMRALL PUBLISHING CO.
P.O. Box 12
South Bend, Indiana 46624

STUDY GUIDE

INDIANA CHRISTIAN UNIVERSITY

DEMONOLOGY & DELIVERANCE II
PRINCIPALITIES & POWERS

TABLE OF CONTENTS

INDIANA CHRISTIAN UNIVERSITY

DEMONOLOGY & DELIVERANCE II
PRINCIPALITIES & POWERS

Lesson 1

INTRODUCTION

READING:

Ephesians 6:12, *For we wrestle not against flesh and blood, but against principalities, against powers, against the rulers of the darkness of this world, against spiritual wickedness in high places.* (See also Matthew 24)

1. CHRISTENDOM AND WESTERN CIVILIZATION IS ENTERING ITS FINAL WARFARE BEFORE ARMAGEDDON

A. It is a time of abundant life, but also of abundant death.

B. It is a time of abundant prosperity, but also of abundant poverty.

C. It is a time of abundant love for God, and great hatred toward God.

D. It is a time of the outpouring of the Holy Spirit, but also of the manifestation of demonic powers.

2. THE ONLY INTELLIGENT WAY TO INTERPRET THESE TIMES ARE BY PROPHETICAL FULFILLMENT

In this study we hope to outline the most historic years of world history and present a Biblical interpretation of our times.

A. This is what Daniel would have done had he lived today.

B. It is the message Jeremiah would preach from every street corner.

C. Ezekiel would proclaim the final conflict by divine interpretation.

Our world is headed for the year 2,000 A.D. in prophecy. The termination of this millennium will conclude the final judgments for sin and rebellion against God and bring in the magnificent millennial reign of our Lord Jesus Christ

3. THE CHALLENGE

Today the church must rise up to the greatest action of its entire history.

Jesus prophesied that His Church shall prevail. In Matthew 16:18, he said, *...upon this rock I will build my church; and the gates of hell shall not prevail against it.*

In these deliverance studies of Principalities and Powers we will be exposing the occult, revealing knowledge of the doctrines, words, rites, eulogies, phrases and definitions that demon worshipers use.

Here is an incomplete list of occult words that we will be studying.

1.   AUGURY: Divination from omens and signs.

2.   AUTOMATIC WRITING: writing under a trance induced by spirit or demon powers; the spirit writes.

3.   ASTROLOGY: Fortune telling by stars or the zodiac.

4.   ASTRAL PROJECTION: Soul leaves the body and travels on a different plane of consciousness.

5.   ANIMISM: Belief that inanimate objects are alive and have souls.

6.   AMULET: Ornament inscribed with a magic spell or sign, usually worn around the neck or wrist.

7.   ALL HALLOWS EVE: October 31, witch festival.

8.   BLACK MAGIC: Form of witchcraft, often called the black arts, using demon power for occult force.

9.   BLACK MASS: A requiem Mass, at which the clergy is dressed in black. It is a blasphemous parody of the Mass by worshipers of Satan.

10. BEWITCH: To influence by witchcraft.

11. CLAIRVOYANT: A medium who forecasts distant happenings through visions.

12. CULT: Religious group, possibly Christian, off doctrinally or spiritually; Satan worshipers.

13. CRYSTAL GAZER: Person who uses a crystal ball for divination.

15. CARTOMANCY: Fortune-telling with cards.

16. CURSE: Incantation for harm to come upon one.

17. COVEN: An assembly of thirteen witches.

18. **CEPHALOMANCY:** Divination using the skull or head of a donkey or goat.

19. **CONJURE:** To summon a departed demon spirit, often by incantation.

20. **CHIROMANCY:** Divination by lines of a person's hand.

21. **DIVINATION:** Foretell future event or discover hidden information.

22. **DEMON:** Evil attendant power of spirit, subservient to Satan.

23. **ENCHANTER:** A sorcerer, one who can cast a spell, as by magic; a witch.

24. **ESBAT:** Witchcraft meeting held for transacting business or to accomplish an act of Satanic mischief.

25. **EXORCISM:** Ritual used to drive away a spirit contrary to exorcist's will.

26. **EXTRA-SENSORY PERCEPTION:** Ability to gain insights without the use of ordinary senses. ESP.

27. **FETISH:** Object regarded magical or sacred.

28. **FAMILIAR SPIRIT:** Spirit embodied in a person which attends, serves and guards a person; spirit can also be in form of a person.

29. **FORTUNE-TELLER:** One who tells future events for individuals.

30. **GRAPHOLOGY:** Analysis of character through one's handwriting.

31. **HOROSCOPE:** Diagram showing position of planets and stars with their signs or the zodiac, used by astrologers for divination.

32. **HEX:** To affect by an evil spell.

33. **MEDIUM:** Person acting as the communicator between this world and the spirit world, with the ability to talk to the dead.

34. **MEDITATION:** Fixing your mind on one object for enlightenment by spirits.

35. **MYSTIC:** One who is into mysticism or occults.

36. **NECROMANCY:** Conjuring spirits of the dead to reveal future events, or to influence them.

37. **OBSERVER OF TIMES:** Same as astrology.

38. **OCCULT:** Secret, mysterious, relating to supernatural forces.

39. **OUIJA BOARD:** Game board used to obtain spiritualistic or telepathic messages about the future or other hidden knowledge.

40. **POLTERGEIST:** Mischievous ghost said to be responsible for strange noises or movement of inanimate objects.

41. POTIONS: Herb mixes, drugs with magical or drug state inducing powers.

42. PSYCHIC PHENOMENA: Events that cannot be explained by physical reference, and are attributed to spiritual forces.

43. PALMISTRY: Divination by means of a wand or stick.

44. RHABDOMANCY: Divination by means of a wand or stick.

45. REINCARNATION: Rebirth of a soul into a new human body or other form of life.

46. SATANISM: Satan worship or idol worship usually involving travesty of Christian rites.

47. SPIRITISM: Belief that departed spirits commune with living people, usually through a medium.

48. SOOTHSAYING: Act of foretelling future events.

49. SEANCE: Group meeting to receive communication from spirits through a medium.

50. SORCERY: Use of power obtained from control of evil spirits.

51. SORCERER: Wizard or witch.

52. SATANIC CHURCH: Refers to any group practicing Satanism.

53. SABBAT: Main meeting of witches to bring in new members.

54. SOUL TRANSMIGRATION: Astral projection; transferring of souls.

55. TALISMAN: A consecrated object, such as a ring or stone, bearing engraved figures or symbols supposed to bring good luck, keep away evil etc.; amulet.

56. TAROT: Fortune-telling cards.

57. VOODOO: Old form of ritual witchcraft usually similar to black magic rituals.

58. WITCH: Woman or man who practices black arts and other types of occult.

59. WIZARD: a male witch who uses spirit power to bring about certain reactions; sorcerer.

60. WITCHDOCTOR: One who uses herbs or machines to cure in non-medical ways.

61. WARLOCK: A male witch

62. WITCHCRAFT: A type of an occult. The word is often used by the press to demote all the occults collectively.

63. YOGA: Exercise and meditation opening the mind to dark powers.

64. ZODIAC: Imaginary belt of planets and constellations forming the astrological signs.

This is only a partial list of occult activities, but will serve to awaken you to the word usage of the occult.

NOTES

INDIANA CHRISTIAN UNIVERSITY

DEMONOLOGY & DELIVERANCE II
PRINCIPALITIES & POWERS

Lesson 2

WHO'S AFRAID OF THE BIG BAD WOLF?

READING:

Isaiah 14:12, *How art thou fallen from heaven, O Lucifer, son of the morning! how art thou cut down to the ground, which didst weaken the nations!*

Ezekiel 28:14, *Thou art the anointed cherub that covereth; and I have set thee so: thou wast upon the holy mountain of God; thou hast walked up and down in the midst of the stones of fire.*

INTRODUCTION:

From the Garden of Eden to the Valley of Jehoshaphat, Satan has taken on a form of frightening proportions. God describes the fallen angel Lucifer in the Bible.

The devil's aliases are many: there are over 200 direct references to him in the Bible.

1. ROARING LION

I Peter 5:8, *Be sober, be vigilant; because your adversary the devil, as a roaring lion, walketh about, seeking whom he may devour.*

2. A SERPENT

Hebrew NACASH—"To hiss, to whisper, to enchant."

A. Genesis 3:1, *Now the serpent was more subtle than any beast of the field which the LORD God had made. And he said unto the woman, Yea, hath God said, Ye shall not eat of every tree of the garden?*

B. II Corinthians 11:3, *But I fear, lest by any means, as the serpent beguiled Eve through his subtlety, so your minds should be corrupted from the simplicity that is in Christ.*

3. THE PRINCE OF DEVILS OR DEMONS—BEELZEBUB

Matthew 12:24, But when the Pharisees heard it, they said, This fellow doth not cast out devils, but by Beelzebub the prince of the devils.

4. THE ENEMY

Matthew 13:28-29, *He said unto them, An enemy hath done this. The servants said unto him, Wilt thou then that we go and gather them up?*

v. 29, *But he said, Nay; lest while ye gather up the tares, ye root up also the wheat with them.*

5. THE DEVIL

Diabolos, the Greek word meaning accuser, slanderer. He slandered Job.

Job 1:6-11, *Now there was a day when the sons of God came to present themselves before the LORD, and Satan came also among them.*

v. 7, *And the LORD said unto Satan, Whence comest thou? Then Satan answered the LORD, and said, From going to and fro in the earth, and from walking up and down in it.*

v. 8, *And the LORD said unto Satan, Hast thou considered my servant Job, that there is none like him in the earth, a perfect and an upright man, one that feareth God, and escheweth evil?*

v. 9, *Then Satan answered the LORD, and said, Doth Job fear God for nought?*

v. 10, *Hast not thou made an hedge about him, and about his house, and about all that he hath on every side? thou hast blessed the work of his hands, and his substance is increased in the land.*

v. 11, *But put forth thine hand now, and touch all that he hath, and he will curse thee to thy face.*

6. LIAR

A. John 8:44, *Ye are of your father the devil, and the lusts of your father ye will do. He was a murderer from the beginning, and abode not in the truth, because there is no truth in him. When he speaketh a lie, he speaketh of his own: for he is a liar, and the father of it.*

B. Performs lying wonders.

Revelation 16:14, *For they are the spirits of devils, working miracles, which go forth unto the kings of the earth and of the whole world, to gather them to the battle of that great day of God Almighty.*

7. THE CORRUPTER OF MINDS

II Corinthians 11:3, *But I fear, lest by any means, as the serpent beguiled Eve through his subtlety, so your minds should be corrupted from the simplicity that is in Christ.*

8. THE TEMPTER

Matthew 4:3, *And when the tempter came to him, he said, If thou be the Son of God, command that these stones be made bread.*

9. THE ADVERSARY

I Peter 5:8, *Be sober, be vigilant; because your adversary the devil, as a roaring lion, walketh about, seeking whom he may devour.*

10. SATAN—GREEK, SATANAS

Revelation 12:9, *And the great dragon was cast out, that old serpent, called the Devil, and Satan, which deceiveth the whole world: he was cast out into the earth, and his angels were cast out with him.*

11. A DECEIVER

Revelation 20:3, *And cast him into the bottomless pit, and shut him up, and set a seal upon him, that he should deceive the nations no more, till the thousand years should be fulfilled: and after that he must be loosed a little season.*

12. A DRAGON

A. Revelation 12:9, *And the great dragon was cast out, that old serpent, called the Devil, and Satan, which deceiveth the whole world: he was cast out into the earth, and his angels were cast out with him.*

B. Revelation 20:2, *And he laid hold on the dragon, that old serpent, which is the Devil, and Satan, and bound him a thousand years.*

13. THE WICKED ONE

Matthew 13:19, *When any one heareth the word of the kingdom, and understandeth it not, then cometh the wicked one, and catcheth away that which was sown in his heart. This is he which received seed by the way side.*

14. THE GOD OF THIS WORLD

II Corinthians 4:4, *In whom the god of this world hath blinded the minds of them which believe not, lest the light of the glorious gospel of Christ, who is the image of God, should shine unto them.*

15. A PRINCE

A. Ephesians 2:2, *Wherein in time past ye walked according to the course of this world, according to the prince of the power of the air, the spirit that now worketh in the children of disobedience.*

B. Ephesians 6:12, *For we wrestle not against flesh and blood, but against principalities, against powers, against the rulers of the darkness of this world, against spiritual wickedness in high places.*

16. HE IS A KING

Matthew 12:24, *. . .This fellow doth not cast out devils, but by Beelzebub the prince of the devils.*

17. WHO'S AFRAID OF THE BIG BAD WOLF?

A. Modern society is being bombarded by demonic and satanic superstitions and aberrations such as black cats, curses, broken mirrors, time of the moon, astrology and tarot cards.

B. From childhood, boys and girls have heard of the "big bad wolf!"

C. That "bad wolf" was always characterized as being provocative. He was looking for trouble and humans were his target.

That "bad wolf" was a predator. He devoured his enemies. He had no mercy.

18. THE POWERS THAT BE

A. In this lesson we are studying about the devil, Satan and his fallen angels as Principalities and Powers of the nether world.

B. It is time the Church of Jesus Christ shows this generation it is not afraid of evil of any category.

19. HOW CAN THE CHURCH TEACH THE WORLD TO BE UNAFRAID?

A. The Church must know its arsenal.

B. The Church must know its enemy.

C. The Church must recognize this enemy and his works.

    D. The Church must be willing to face her enemy to do battle with him.

    E. The Church must know that Jesus Christ gives His Church power to defeat and destroy that enemy!

        1) Matthew 16:18, *. . .upon this rock I will build my church; and the gates of hell shall not prevail against it.*

        2) John 10:10, *The thief cometh not, but for to steal, and to kill, and to destroy: I am come that they might have life, and they might have it more abundantly.*

        The Church possesses the full capacity of God's power. The enemy is totally destroyed.

20. GOD'S WORD SAYS THAT THE THIEF IS THE DEVIL—HE IS THE BIG BAD WOLF

As a thief the devil wants to:

A. Steal your relationship with God. He does this by keeping you from reading the promises of the Bible. It is this divine truth which sets you free.

John 8:36, *If the son therefore shall make you free, ye shall be free indeed.*

B. Steal your testimony. The devil wants to keep you from giving your witness and winning others to Christ.

C. Steal our spiritual strength, keep us as defeated and discouraged disciples, and hinder us from being delivered in the day of battle.

D. Keep us from being healed.

E. Keep us from joy and peace.

F. Steal our prosperity, and keep us from possessing our possessions. This thief wants to steal everything from us that came to us from Jesus Christ. The thief wants us to get involved in things that are not of God and that are not profitable to spirituality.

21. THE CHRISTIAN'S REFUGE

A. Unless the Christian remains obedient to the will of God, by staying in the Word, the devil can trap him. It will be like a fly being caught in a spider web, all tangled up.

B. <u>There is perfect safety for all Christians.</u> There is a way out of any situation. There is an answer and that is found in the Word of God.

   1) John 10:10, *The thief cometh not, but for to steal, and to kill, and to destroy: I am come that they might have life, and that they might have it more abundantly.*

   2) Romans 8:37-39, *Nay, in all these things we are more than conquerors through him that loved us.*

     v. 38, *For I am persuaded, that neither death, nor life, nor angels, nor principalities, nor powers, nor things present, nor things to come,*

     v. 39, *Nor height, nor depth, nor any other creature, shall be able to separate us from the love of God, which is in Christ Jesus our Lord.*

   3) II Timothy 1:7, *For God hath not given us the spirit of fear; but of power, and of love, and of a sound mind.*

   4) I John 4:4, *Ye are of God, little children, and have overcome them: because greater is he that is in you, than he that is in the world.*

22. CHRISTIANS HAVE THE POWER TO DESTROY THE ENEMY

A. Jesus tells us to be obedient and stay in the Word. There is freedom in the Word of God.

John 8:31-32, *Then said Jesus to those Jews which believed on him, If ye continue in my word, then are ye my disciples indeed;*

v. 32, *And ye shall know the truth, and the truth shall make you free.*

B. By the power of the Holy Spirit filling us, we have the power to destroy the enemy.

Isaiah 59:19, *So shall they fear the name of the LORD from the west, and his glory from the rising of the sun. When the enemy shall come in like a flood, the spirit of the LORD shall lift up a standard against him.*

C. Jesus assures us again:

John 15:7, *If ye abide in me, and my words abide in you, ye shall ask what ye will, and it shall be done unto you.*

D. Nowhere in the Bible does God infer that we should fear the devil. The opposite is true.

James 4:7, *Submit yourselves therefore to God. Resist the devil, and he will flee from you.*

Let him run! As God's children, we are unafraid.

23. THE ULTIMATE DESTINY OF THE BIG BAD WOLF

Revelation 20:1-3, *And I saw an angel come down from heaven, having the key of the bottomless pit and a great chain in his hand.*

v. 2, *And he laid hold on the dragon, that old serpent, which is the Devil, and Satan, and bound him a thousand years,*

v. 3, *And cast him into the bottomless pit, and shut him up, and set a seal upon him, that he should deceive the nations no more, till the thousand years should be fulfilled: and after that he must be loosed a little season.*

NOTES

INDIANA CHRISTIAN UNIVERSITY

DEMONS & DELIVERANCE II
PRINCIPALITIES & POWERS

Lesson 3

WHAT DOES GOD SAY ABOUT PRINCIPALITIES AND POWERS?

READING:

Titus 3:1, *Put them in mind to be subject to principalities and powers, to obey magistrates, to be ready to every good work.*

INTRODUCTION:

God knows the subject of principalities and powers. He witnessed Lucifer, the archangel of praise and worship, become a potentate of evil principalities and sinful power.

1.   GOD SAYS THAT CHRIST IS THE CREATOR OF ALL POWER

Colossians 1:16, *For by him were all things created, that are in heaven, and that are in earth, visible and invisible, whether they be thrones, or dominions, or principalities, or powers: all things were created by him, and for him.*

2.   GOD SAYS CHRIST IS THE HEAD OF ALL POWER

God elevated Christ above all principalities and powers.

Colossians 2:10, *And ye are complete in him, which is the head of all principality and power.*

Ephesians 1:21, *Far above all principality, and power, and might, and dominion, and every name that is named, not only in this world, but also in that which is to come.*

3.   GOD SAYS THAT CHRIST DESTROYED THE DEVIL'S POWER

Colossians 2:15, *And having spoiled principalities and powers, he made a shew of them openly, triumphing over them in it.*

4. GOD REVEALS WISDOM TO THE CHURCH

Ephesians 3:10, *To the intent that now unto the principalities and powers in heavenly places might be known by the church the manifold wisdom of God.*

5. GOD REVEALS THE BELIEVER'S POSITION IN POWER

Romans 8:37-39, *Nay, in all these things we are more than conquerors through him that loved us.*

v. 38, *For I am persuaded, that neither death, nor life, nor angels, nor principalities, nor powers, nor things present, nor things to come,*

v. 39, *Nor height, nor depth, nor any other creature, shall be able to separate us from the love of God, which is in Christ Jesus our Lord.*

6. GOD WANTS BELIEVERS TO UNDERSTAND PRINCIPALITIES

Ephesians 3:10, *To the intent that now unto the principalities and powers in heavenly places might be known by the church the manifold wisdom of God.*

7. GOD SAYS THIS IS THE ARMOR

Ephesians 6:10, *Finally, my brethren, be strong in the Lord, and in the power of his might.*

8. GOD WANTS THE BELIEVERS TO KNOW THE BATTLE IS WITH PRINCIPALITIES AND POWERS

Ephesians 6:12 in eight translations:

1) *For we wrestle not against flesh and blood, but against principalities, against powers, against the rulers of the darkness of this world, against spiritual wickedness in high places.*

—King James Version

2) *Ours is not a conflict with mere flesh and blood; but with the depotisms; the empires, the forces that control and govern this dark world: the spiritual hosts of evil arrayed against us in heavenly warfare.*

—Weymouth

3) *The adversaries with whom we wrestle are not flesh and blood, but they are principalities, the powers, and the sovereigns of this present darkness, the spirits of evil in the heavens.*

—Conybeare

4) *We have to struggle, not with blood and flesh, but with the Angelic rulers, the Angelic authorities, the Potentates of the dark present, the*

spirit-forces of evil in the heavenly sphere; so take God's armour; praying...with all manner of prayer.

—Dr. James Moffatt

5) *For we are not contending against flesh and blood, but against the principalities, against the powers, against the world rulers of this present darkness, against the spiritual hosts of wickedness in the heavenly places.*

—Revised Standard Version

6) *For our fight is not against any physical enemy: it is against organizations and powers that are spiritual. We are up against the unseen power that controls this dark world, and spiritual agents from the very headquarters of evil.*

—Phillips Modern English

7) *Put on the armour which God precedes, so that you may be able to stand firm against the devices of the devil. For our fight is not against human foes, but against cosmic powers, against the authorities and potentates of this dark world, against the superhuman forces of evil in the heavens.*

—New English Bible

8) *For we do not wrestle against flesh and blood, but against principalities, against powers, against the rulers of the darkness of this age, against spiritual wickedness in the heavenly places.*

—The New King James Version

9. GOD SAYS PRINCIPALITIES REINFORCE THEIR BATTLE FOR SOULS

A. Luke 11:24-26, *When the unclean spirit is gone out of a man, he walketh through dry places, seeking rest; and finding none, he saith, I will return unto my house whence I came out.*

v. 25, *And when he cometh, he findeth it swept and garnished.*

v. 26, *Then goeth he, and taketh to him seven other spirits more wicked than himself; and they enter in, and dwell there: and the last state of that man is worse than the first.*

B. You can say, "Go into space," because Satan is the prince of the power of the air.

Ephesians 2:2, *Wherein in time past ye walked according to the course of this world, according to the prince of the power of the air, the spirit that now worketh in the children of disobedience.*

10. GOD WARNS HUMANS AGAINST PRINCIPALITIES AND POWERS

Deuteronomy 18:9-12, *When thou art come into the land which the LORD thy God giveth thee, thou shalt not learn to do after the abominations of those nations. There shall not be found among you any one that . . .*

1) *maketh his son or his daughter to pass through the fire,* (A heathen religious ritual)

2) *or that useth divination,* (Seeking supernatural guidance, especially regarding the future)

3) *or an observer of times,*

4) *or an enchanter,*

5) *or a witch,*

6) *or a charmer*

7) *or a consulter with familiar spirits,*

8) *or a wizard,*

9) *or a necromancer* (conjuring spirits of the dead)

For all that do these things are an abomination unto the LORD: and because of these abominations the LORD thy God doth drive them out from before thee.

11. GOD WARNS HUMANS AGAINST DEMON-INSPIRED LEADERS

The Bible has several names for humans who give themselves over to satanic works, operations and activities.

False christs or antichrists—imitators and pretenders who claim to be the Messiah. Jesus warned His followers not be deceived by them.

A. False Christs

Matthew 24:24, *For there shall arise false christs, and false prophets, and shall shew great signs and wonders; insomuch that, if it were possible, they shall deceive the very elect* (God's chosen ones).

B. False Prophets—Any person claiming to possess a message from God, but not possessing a divine commission, nor displaying genuine fruit. Matthew 7:15, *Beware of false prophets, which come to you in sheep's* clothing, but inwardly they are ravening wolves.

Matthew 24:11, *And many false prophets shall rise, and shall deceive many.*

C. False Teachers—Any person claiming to be a genuine teacher of God, but not possessing a divine commission, nor displaying genuine fruit.

1) They teach heresy.

II Peter 2:1-2, *But there were false prophets also among the people, even as there shall be false teachers among you, who privily shall bring in damnable heresies, even denying the Lord that bought them, and bring upon themselves swift destruction.*

v.2, *And many shall follow their pernicious ways; by reason of whom the way of truth shall be evil spoken of.*

2) They are covetous and flattering.

II Peter 2:3, *And through covetousness shall they with feigned words make merchandise of you: whose judgment now of a long time lingereth not, and their damnation slumbereth not.*

3) They are lustful and adulterous.

II Peter 2:10, 14, *But chiefly them that walk after the flesh in the lust of uncleanness, and despise government. Presumptuous are they, self-willed, they are not afraid to speak evil of dignities.*

v. 14, *Having eyes full of adultery, and that cannot cease from sin;...*

4) They are rebellious.

II Peter 2:10, *. . .Presumptuous are they, self-willed, they are not afraid to speak evil of dignities*

5) They speak evil of things they do not understand.

II Peter 2:12, *But these, as natural beasts, made to be taken and destroyed, speak evil of the things that they understand not; and shall utterly perish in their own corruption.*

6) They are riotous.

II Peter 2:13, *And shall receive the reward of unrighteousness, as they that count it pleasure to riot in the day time. Spots they are and blemishes, sporting themselves with their own deceivings while they feast with you.*

7) They are deceiving.

II Peter 2:14, *Having eyes full of adultery, and that cannot cease from sin; beguiling unstable souls: an heart they have exercised with covetous practices; cursed children.*

8) They are vain.

II Peter 2:18, *For when they speak great swelling words of vanity, they allure through the lusts of the flesh, through much wantonness, those that were clean escaped from them who live in error.*

9) They live in error.

II Peter 2:19, *While they promise them liberty, they themselves are the servants of corruption: for of whom a man is overcome, of the same is he brought in bondage.*

10) They promise liberty, but live in corruption (II Peter 2:19).

11) They were saved but have fallen from grace and returned to uncleanness and are overcome.

II Peter 2:20, *For if after they have escaped the pollutions of the world through the knowledge of the Lord and Saviour Jesus Christ, they are again entangled therein, and overcome, and latter end is worse with them than the beginning.*

II Thessalonians 2:9-11, *Even him,* (the lawless one, the Antichrist), *whose coming is after the working of Satan with all power and signs and lying wonders,*

v. 10, *And will all deceivableness of unrighteousness in them that perish; because they received not the love of the truth, that they might be saved.*

v. 11, *And for this cause God shall send them strong delusion, that they should believe a lie.*

I John 4:1-3, *Beloved, believe not every spirit, but try the spirits whether they are of God: because many false prophets are gone out into the world.*

v. 2, *Hereby know ye the Spirit of God: Every spirit that confesseth that Jesus Christ is come in the flesh is of God:*

v. 3, *And every spirit that confesseth not that Jesus Christ is come in the flesh is not of God: and this is that spirit of antichrist, whereof ye have heard that it should come; and even now already is it in the world.*

Revelation 13:13-14, *And he doeth great wonders, so that he maketh fire come down from heaven on the earth in the sight of men,*

v. 14, *And deceiveth them that dwell on the earth by means of those miracles which he had power to do in the sight of the beast; saying to them that dwell on the earth, that they should make an image to the beast, which had the wound by a sword, and did live.*

12. WHO ARE DECEIVED BY PRINCIPALITIES AND POWERS

Revelation 16:14, *For they are the spirits of devils, working miracles, which go forth unto the kings* (rulers and leaders) *of the earth and of the whole world, to gather them to the battle of that great day of God Almighty.*

NOTES

INDIANA CHRISTIAN UNIVERSITY

DEMONOLOGY & DELIVERANCE II
PRINCIPALITIES & POWERS

Lesson 4

WHY DO MILLIONS OF PEOPLE SEEK DEMON POWER TODAY?

READING:

Isaiah 8:19, *And when they shall say unto you, Seek unto them that have familiar spirits, and unto wizards that peep, and that mutter: Should not a people seek unto their God? for the living to the dead?* (KJV)

Isaiah 8:19, *And when the people* (instead of putting their trust in God) *shall say to you, Consult for direction mediums and wizards who chirp and mutter: Should not a people seek and consult their God? Should they consult the dead on behalf of the living?* (The Amp. Bible)

INTRODUCTION:

There is an amazing and remarkable revival of demon power in this country. There is great publicity in the mass media about it.

The Bible reveals the absolute truth about the world of the supernatural, and especially the spirit world. According to Jesus, Peter, Paul, James and John, there are demons and evil spirits.

1. **THE VERY CORE OF THE OCCULT IS A QUEST FOR SUPER-NATURAL POWER:**

   A. Every witch doctor seeks great power.

   B. Every wizard seeks to know the unknown.

   C. This is power outside of God—other than holiness or purity.

2. AN ANGEL BECAME A DEVIL SEEKING POWER

A. Isaiah 14:12-17, *How art thou fallen from heaven, O Lucifer, son of the morning! how art thou cut down to the ground, which didst weaken the nations!*

v. 13, *For thou hast said in thine heart, I will ascend into heaven, I will exalt my throne above the stars of God: I will sit also upon the mount of the congregation, in the sides of the north:*

v. 14, *I will ascend above the heights of the clouds; I will be like the most High.*

v. 15, *Yet thou shalt be brought down to hell, to the sides of the pit.*

v. 16, *They that see thee shall narrowly look upon thee, and consider thee, saying, Is this the man that made the earth to tremble, and did shake kingdoms.*

v. 17, *That made the world as a wilderness, and destroyed the cities thereof; that opened not the house of his prisoners?*

B. Ezekiel 28:14-19, *Thou art the anointed cherub that covereth; and I have set thee so: thou wast upon the holy mountain of God; thou hast walked up and down in the midst of the stones of fire.*

v. 15, *Thou wast perfect in thy ways from the day that thou wast created, till iniquity was found in thee.*

v. 16, *By the multitude of thy merchandise they have filled the midst of thee with violence, and thou has sinned: therefore I will cast thee as profane out of the mountain of God: and I will destroy thee, O covering cherub, from the midst of the stones of fire.*

v. 17, *Thine heart was lifted up because of thy beauty, thou hast corrupted thy wisdom by reason of thy brightness: I will cast thee to the ground, I will lay thee before kings, that they may behold thee.*

v. 18, *Thou hast defiled thy sanctuaries by the multitude of thine iniquities, by the iniquity of thy traffick; therefore will I bring forth a fire from the midst of thee, it shall devour thee, and I will bring thee to ashes upon the earth in the sight of all them that behold thee.*

v. 19, *All they that know thee among the people shall be astonished at thee: thou shalt be a terror, and never shalt thou be any more.*

So the reason why people engage in demonic activities is that they are seeking illegitimate power.

3. IN THE OCCULT THE RULING QUEST IS TO CONTROL OTHERS

A. The heart of the occult is to control fellow men by fear, superstition, curses and lies.

B. The desire is control, to be an aristocrat and to direct others.

4. ESCAPE FROM PROBLEMS AND TROUBLES

A. There are millions who turn their lives over to gurus and cults because of big problems in their lives. They seek release without repentance.

B. The deceiving spirits claim to answer their questions about life.

5. ESCAPE FROM INSECURITY

A. Millions of people can't stand up to the strain, the wear, and the fear of life. They feel like failures.

B. Demon power is an escape from reality. It is like alcohol or drugs. However, you must come back and face life!

6. SOME BECOME POSSESSED BY AN INORDINATE DESIRE TO KNOW THE UNKNOWN: OFTENTIMES IT IS FORBIDDEN KNOW-LEDGE

A. A major entrance into the mind and soul of the possessed in this country is the subtle and often considered harmless pursuit of seeking to know the unknown.

B. Multitudes of people ensnared in the occult began with a game like the ouija board or tarot cards and ended up becoming warlocks.

C. Many people began by reading their astrological prognostications which later led into yoga, oriental meditation, and later into either white or black magic.

D. There might be various methods for Satan to lead different individuals, but the end is to deceive innocent people into demonic activity and to possess them.

7. FASTING AND PRAYING FOR DEMON POWER

In the Western World, we do not realize the intensity of fervor used by witch doctors, warlocks and astrologers.

8. IN RUSSIA

The charlatan Rasputin held the royal family of Russia under his magnetic powers. He deceived them by demon force. He was partly to blame for the fall of the czar.

9. THE GURU

The guru opens the immortal doors of his soul to the expanses of heavenly forces operated by the former archangel and now a king of demons.

10. FOR POWER

A. The palm reader says, "I know more than you. For money I will tell you all about it."

B. The crystal ball is a tool for gaining power.

C. Knowledge is power.

D. Money is power.

11. MOTHER EVE

Mother Eve thought she was coming into a power of knowledge, yet she lost all and cried, "The serpent has deceived me."

12. PAUL REBUKED BAR-JESUS (ELYMAS)

Acts 13:6-12, *And when they had gone through the isle unto Paphos, they found a certain sorcerer, a false prophet, a Jew, whose name was Bar-jesus:*

v. 7, *Which was with the deputy of the country, Sergius Paulus, a prudent man; who called for Barnabas and Saul, and desired to hear the word of God.*

v. 8, *But Elymas the sorcerer (for so is his name by interpretation) withstood them, seeking to turn away the deputy from the faith.*

v. 9, *Then Saul, (who also is called Paul), filled with the Holy Ghost, set his eyes on him,*

v. 10, *And said, O full of all subtlety and all mischief, thou child of the devil, thou enemy of all righteousness, wilt thou not cease to pervert the right ways of the Lord?*

v. 11, *And now, behold, the hand of the Lord is upon thee, and thou shalt be blind, not seeing the sun for a season. And immediately there fell on him a mist and a darkness; and he went about seeking some to lead him by the hand.*

v. 12, *Then the deputy, when he saw what was done, believed, being astonished at the doctrine of the Lord.*

Paul accused Bar-jesus of being full of mischief, a child of the devil, and an enemy of righteousness.

13. THE CHRISTIAN'S QUEST FOR POWER IS GOD'S POWER

A. To heal

B. To lift burdens

C. To be enriched in God

D. To be unselfish

14. THE BURDEN OF THE OCCULT

A. One of the means of seeking power is by the use of drugs. By the use of psychedelic drugs, the human brain is tormented and sometimes destroyed. The counter-culture bears a heavy burden of privation, of misunderstanding, and often of rejection.

B. Drugs become our unreasonable unbelief which sets a human personally against society and against the world of which we are a part.

C. The occult makes harsh demands of its victims. It causes unreasonable decisions regarding behavior, and long-term consequences to its victims. It is a big price to pay for deception.

15. THE DEVIL IS NEVER SATISFIED

It is not on record that the devil has ever been satisfied or satisfied anyone who follows him. He makes the human greedy for more. He always promises more than he ever gives.

16. WHAT CAUSED THAT VACUUM OF SEEKING POWER?

A. Man's thirst is not quenched.

B. The church does not present Christ in a full manner so as to quench a man's thirst for knowledge and power.

C. Most evils come because they are not resisted—not revealed. "When good men do nothing, evil prevails."

D. The human respects power and sometimes worships power. Notice how men pray, "Almighty God. . ."

Jesus said, ". . .pray, our Father. . ."

NOTES

INDIANA CHRISTIAN UNIVERSITY

DEMONOLOGY & DELIVERANCE II
PRINCIPALITIES & POWERS

Lesson 5

BABYLON'S SORCERERS AND WIZARDS

READING:

Daniel 2:1, *And in the second year of the reign of Nebuchadnezzar, Nebuchadnezzar dreamed dreams, wherewith his spirit was troubled, and his sleep brake from him.*

v. 2, *Then the king commanded to call the magicians, and the astrologers, and the sorcerers, and the Chaldeans, for to shew the king his dreams. So they came and stood before the king.*

GOD'S PLAN OF THE AGES—

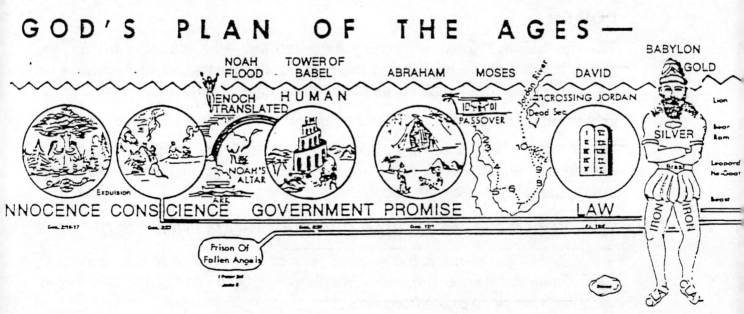

INTRODUCTION:

There is always a beginning place for everything.

    A. From Adam to Noah, it seems that the sins were more of the flesh and soul; *marrying and giving in marriage, eating and drinking.*

    B. From Adam to Noah, which was only 10 generations, and the average person spans five generations (that is from his grandfather to his grandsons), the direction of sin moved from the flesh to the spirit. This is very important!

    C. The Tower of Babel was a spirit rebellion against God. Man was saying that even if a flood does reoccur, we will save ourselves.

    The empire of Babylon was built on the ruins of the Tower of Babel. In this first world empire we find demon power in great manifestation. It is truly amazing that man had turned from light to darkness.

        1) He had turned from truth to lies.

        2) He had turned from love to hate.

        3) He had turned from the Creator to the destroyer.

        4) Man was not guided by the devil.

1. BABYLON'S KING NEBUCHADNEZZAR RESORTED TO DEMON POWER

The devil always seeks to destroy the head first—the leader, the king, the priest. It was not the misfits and the chronic pessimists, but the emperor on his throne given over to all forms of demon manifestations and worship.

One group, "The Chaldeans," were a special local breed of soothsayers.

Daniel 2:2, *Then the king commanded to call the magicians, and the astrologers, and the sorcerers, and the Chaldeans, for to shew the king his dreams. so they came and stood before the king.*

2. THE WORLD DICTATOR WAS GIVEN A DREAM FROM GOD

    A. Daniel 2:1, *And in the second year of the reign of Nebuchadnezzar, Nebuchadnezzar dreamed dreams, wherewith his spirit was troubled, and his sleep brake from him.*

    The king knew the dream was unusual and important, because *his sleep brake from him.*

B. The king knew of a better way.

Nebuchadnezzar knew Daniel and Hananiah, Mishael and Azariah, the young Israelites from Palestine.

Daniel 1:17-20, *As for these four children, God gave them knowledge and skill in all learning and wisdom: and Daniel had understanding in all visions and dreams.*

v. 18, *Now at the end of the days that the king had said he should bring them in, then the prince of the eunuchs brought them in before Nebuchadnezzar.*

v. 19, *And the king communed with them; and among them all was found none like Daniel, Hananiah, Mishael, and Azariah: therefore stood they before the king.*

v. 20, *And in all matters of wisdom and understanding that the king inquired of them, he found them ten times better than all the magicians and astrologers that were in all his realm.*

C. Yet the Emperor of the whole earth, when he became mystified by a dream, which he had now forgotten, he called for:

1) The magicians of Babylon.

2) The astrologers of the Royal Court.

3) The sorcerers from the witches' coven.

4) The Chaldeans from the ESP of the upper echelon of Babylonian society.

He demanded them to reveal the unknown and to explain the forgotten dream.

D. The King threatened the magicians.

Daniel 2:5, *The king answered and said to the Chaldeans, The thing is gone from me: if ye will not make known unto me the dream, with the interpretation thereof, ye shall be cut in pieces, and your houses shall be made a dunghill.*

E. King Nebuchadnezzar knew the qualities of these evil men.

Daniel 2:9, *But if ye will not make known unto me the dream, there is but one decree for you: for ye have prepared lying and corrupt words to speak before me, till the time be changed: therefore tell me the dream, and I shall know that ye can shew me the interpretation thereof.*

3. THE DEVIL'S REBUTTAL

He is always a counterfeiter:

Daniel 2:10-11, *The Chaldeans answered before the king, and said, There is not a man upon the earth that can shew the king's matter: therefore there is no king, lord, nor ruler, that asked such things at any magician, or astrologer, or Chaldean.*

v. 11, *And it is a rare thing that the king requireth, and there is none other that can shew it before the king, except the gods, whose dwelling is not with flesh.*

The devil is very conscious of all his limitations. The church must know the devil's limitations also.

4. GOD'S ANSWER TO BABYLONIAN WITCHCRAFT

Daniel 2:27-35, *Daniel answered in the presence of the king, and said, The secret which the king hath demanded cannot the wise men, the astrologers, the magicians, the soothsayers, shew unto the king;*

v. 28, *But there is a God in heaven that revealeth secrets, and maketh known to the king Nebuchadnezzar what shall be in the latter days. Thy dream, and the visions of thy head upon thy bed, are these;*

v. 29, *As for thee, O king, thy thoughts came into thy mind upon thy bed, what should come to pass hereafter: and he that revealeth secrets maketh known to thee what shall come to pass.*

v. 30, *But as for me, this secret is not revealed to me for any wisdom that I have more than any living, but for their sakes that shall make known the interpretation to the king, and that thou mightest know the thoughts of thy heart.*

v. 31, *Thou, O king, sawest, and behold a great image. This great image, whose brightness was excellent, stood before thee; and the form thereof was terrible.*

v. 32, *This image's head was of fine gold, his breast and his arms of silver, his belly and his thighs of brass.*

v. 33, *His legs of iron, his feet part of iron and part of clay.*

v. 34, *Thou sawest till that a stone was cut out without hands, which smote the image upon his feet that were of iron and clay, and brake them to pieces.*

v. 35, *Then was the iron, the clay, the brass, the silver, and the gold, broken to pieces together, and became like the chaff of the summer threshing floors; and the wind carried them away, that no place was found for them: and the stone that smote the image became a great mountain, and filled the whole earth.*

5. FROM THE BEGINNING OF TIME, THE DEVIL HAS BEEN MEDDLING IN WORLD AFFAIRS

A. He does not have the final answers. No demonical phenomena, such as Hitler or Alexander the Great, have had the right answer to man's problems.

B. Also the witch is one who practices sorcery by magic, by using oracular formulas, incantations and strange mutterings.

C. In Egypt it can be the ANHK or deep studies into Pyramidology.

D. In the Arab world it can be the "evil eye." Whatever form, it is forbidden of God.

6. THE RESULTS

Daniel 2:47-48, *The king answered unto Daniel, and said, Of a truth it is, that your God is a God of gods, and a Lord of kings, and a revealer of secrets, seeing thou couldest reveal this secret.*

v. 48, *Then the king made Daniel a great man, and gave him many great gifts, and made him ruler over the whole province of Babylon, and chief of the governors over all the wise men of Babylon.*

7. GOD WARNS BABYLON

Isaiah 47:1, 9, *Come down, and sit in the dust, O virgin daughter of Babylon, sit on the ground; there is no throne, O daughter of the Chaldeans: for thou shalt no more be called tender and delicate.*

v. 9, *But these two things shall come to thee in a moment in one day, the loss of children, and widowhood; they shall come upon thee in their perfection for the multitude of the sorceries, and for the great abundance of thine enchantments.*

Babylon fell because of her witchcraft. Babylon refused the God of Daniel.

8. BABYLONIAN SORCERY IS ALIVE TODAY

Also, we must know that the sorcery and wizardry of Babylon is alive today, and is to be contested by God's people.

Jeremiah 27:9, *Therefore hearken not ye to your prophets, nor to your diviners, nor to your dreamers, nor to your enchanters, nor to your sorcerers, which speak unto you, saying, Ye shall not serve the king of Babylon.*

God had said they would go into bondage for their transgressions.

9. HOW DOES THE SORCERY WORK?

A. The term sorcerer from the Latin *sors,* "a lot," means one who throws or declares a lot. It is like throwing dice.

B. Sorcery functions in prognostication. It includes the entire field of divinatory occultism.

C. Sorcery includes necromancy, which classifies as a type of sorcery.

D. What God said about the wizards.

1) A wizard is one skilled in magic. He is a sorcerer.

2) The wizard (Heb. *yid 'oni*) is properly, "the knowing or the wise one." Like the "familiar spirit" (Heb. *'ob*), it means in the first instance the alleged "spirit of a deceased person" (actually the divining demon). Then it came to mean him or her who divines by such a spirit or demon.

3) Therefore, both terms mean the divining spirit, and the medium through whom the demon divines. The two concepts, "the divining spirit" and "the divining medium" are frequently so closely identified as to be thought of as one, as in Leviticus 19:31; 20:6.

4) In the Hebrew "unto them that have familiar spirits." The same is true of the term "wizard." Implicit in its meaning is the thought of the wise and knowing demon, the clever and cunning medium, who is skillful in oracular science because the intelligent spirit is in him.

5) It is a super-human knowledge of the spirit inhabiting the human body that makes a spiritistic medium a wizard.

10. GOD'S WORD SAYS:

A. Leviticus 19:31, *Regard not them that have familiar spirits, neither seek after wizards, to be defiled by them: I am the LORD your God.*

B. Leviticus 20:6, *And the soul that turneth after such as have familiar spirits, and after wizards, to go a-whoring after them, I will even set my face against that soul, and will cut him off from among his people.*

C. The seriousness of this sin is seen in Leviticus 20:27, *A man also or woman that hath a familiar spirit, or that is a wizard, shall be put to death: they shall stone them with stones: their blood shall be upon them.*

D. Deuteronomy 18:11, *Or a charmer, or a consulter with familiar spirits, or a wizard, or a necromancer.*

E. I Samuel 28:3, *Now Samuel was dead, and all Israel had lamented him, and buried him in Ramah, even in his own city. And Saul had put away those that had familiar spirits, and the wizards, out of the land.*

F. II Kings 21:6, *And he made his son pass through the fire, and observed times, and used enchantments, and dealt with familiar spirits and wizards: he wrought much wickedness in the sight of the LORD, to provoke him to anger.*

G. II Chronicles 33:6, *And he caused his children to pass through the fire in the valley of the son of Hinnom: also he observed times, and used enchantments, and used witchcraft, and dealt with a familiar spirit, and with wizards: he wrought much evil in the sight of the LORD, to provoke him to anger.*

H. The great prophet Isaiah warned in Isaiah 8:19, *And when they shall say unto you, Seek unto them that have familiar spirits, and unto wizards that peep, and that mutter: should not a people seek unto their God? for the living to the dead?*

This generation must decide between the living God of the Bible, and Babylonian sorcery and wizardry.

NOTES

9. GOD'S JUDGMENT

Leviticus 18:24-30, *Defile not ye yourselves in any of these things: for in all these the nations are defiled which I cast out before you:*

v. 25, *And the land is defiled: therefore I do visit the iniquity thereof upon it, and the land itself vomiteth out her inhabitants.*

v. 26, *Ye shall therefore keep my statutes and my judgments, and shall not commit any of these abominations; neither any of your own nation, nor any stranger that sojourneth among you:*

v. 27, *(For all these abominations have the men of the land done, which were before you, and the land is defiled;)*

v. 28, *That the land spue not you out also, when ye defile it, as it spued out the nations that were before you.*

v. 29, *For whosoever shall commit any of these abominations, even the souls that commit them shall be cut off from among their people.*

v. 30, *Therefore shall ye keep mine ordinance, that ye commit not any one of these abominable customs, which were committed before you, and that ye defile not yourselves therein: I am the LORD your God.*

NOTES

INDIANA CHRISTIAN UNIVERSITY

DEMONOLOGY & DELIVERANCE II
PRINCIPALITIES & POWERS

Lesson 6

SEX AND SATANIC RITUAL

READING:

Exodus 32:1,5-6,8,25,   *And when the people saw that Moses delayed to come down out of the mount, the people gathered themselves together unto Aaron, and said unto him, Up, make us gods, which shall go before us; for as for this Moses, the man that brought us up out of the land of Egypt, we wot not what is become of him.*

v. 5,   *And when Aaron saw it, he built an altar before it; and Aaron made proclamation, and said, Tomorrow is a feast to the LORD.*

v. 6,   *And they rose up early on the morrow, and offered burnt offerings, and brought peace offerings; and the people sat down to eat and to drink, and rose up to play.*

v. 8,   *They have turned aside quickly out of the way which I commanded them: they have made them a molten calf, and have worshipped it, and have sacrificed thereunto, and said, These be thy gods, O Israel, which have brought thee up out of the land of Egypt.*

v. 25,   *And when Moses saw that the people were naked; (for Aaron had made them naked unto their shame among their enemies:)*

INTRODUCTION:

Almost all demon manifestation relates itself in some way to sex. There are far more women and girls abused by Satan than men and boys, yet there are many of them also.

For sure, demon entities manipulate the baser sexual excitement in its victims.

1. ## THE REASON WHY SATAN INVOLVES SEX IN DEMON WORSHIP AND POSSESSION

Eve was the first human to fall prey to, and to be tempted by, Lucifer, the Devil, Satan.

God prophesied that her seed would bruise, destroy, and cancel all the power that the devil had gained by man's transgression.

Genesis 3:4-5, *And the serpent said unto the woman, Ye shall not surely die:*

v. 5, *For God doth know that in the day ye eat thereof, then your eyes shall be opened, and ye shall be as gods, knowing good and evil.*

Genesis 3:15, *And I will put enmity between thee and the woman, and between thy seed and her seed; it shall bruise thy head, and thou shalt bruise his heel.*

Retaliation against the woman is what the devil is seeking to perpetrate upon mankind. In every way, the devil seeks to make woman a slave.

2. ## CLARITA VILLANUEVA

The spirit had intercourse with her. The doctors were witnesses to this.

3. ## THE BOY WHO DISAPPEARED

A girl spirit came to him.

4. ## SAM JEVARATNUM

Sam Jevaratnum of India saw a girl on the road. He rebuked the devil and there was no girl.

5. ## SATANIST CHURCH IN SAN FRANCISCO

They put a nude woman on the altar.

6. ## INITIATION INTO THE OCCULT

This is often by intercourse.

7. ## WOMAN IN RIO DE JANEIRO

She choked her husband in church.

8. ## SUZIE CARRILO

She said her demon killed her husband. The spirit said the husband could not have sex with his wife.

INDIANA CHRISTIAN UNIVERSITY

DEMONOLOGY & DELIVERANCE II
PRINCIPALITIES & POWERS

Lesson 7

THE MYSTERY OF REINCARNATION

READING:

Hebrews 9:27, *And as it is appointed unto men once to die, but after this the judgment.*

INTRODUCTION:

This study is important as it decides human destiny. A believer in reincarnation will fit his life to the doctrine.

1. WHAT IS REINCARNATION?

A. Reincarnation is the philosophy of successive rebirth on this planet.

B. Reincarnation teaches the wheel of eternally recurring birth and death.

C. Reincarnation teaches that human lives are without beginning and ending.

D. Reincarnation teaches that the human souls of planet earth successively return to new forms and bodies. It can be an animal, insect, bird or a human person.

E. Karma is the force which makes each rebirth depend upon previous deeds in other lives.

2. WHERE DID THE DOCTRINE OF REINCARNATION ORIGINATE?

A. The doctrine of reincarnation originated with the devil. His demons, who were originally angels in heaven, are ageless, sexless, and deathless. In one generation a certain demon spirit might possess a Babylonian, still in another generation the same spirit could possess a Sodomite in Sodom.

B. When these spirits speak through a possessed person, they tell of their recurring possessions of human persons.

A person listening to these demons could think it's the man or woman themselves, not knowing it is an evil spirit talking.

This begins the deception. The spirit, for example, can say, "I lived in a French doctor in the 17th century whose name was Jacques. I committed a murder and was never found out and I feel condemned."

C. The possessed person of this generation could say "Oh, that's when I lived before."

The person has not lived before. Rather, a deceiving spirit in him which has possessed another entity in some former time is now speaking out.

D. I met a spiritist in Brazil who had spirits in him that had lived in Napoleon the Great. They could describe his actions and desires and voice intonation. The demon possessed Brazilian would surmise that he was the reincarnation of Napoleon.

E. In several countries of the world we have met demon possessed people who said they were the reimbodiment of those who have lived in other generations.

F. Therefore, it is clear that the doctrine of reincarnation began with the devil. Its field of operation is mostly in pagan persons who are ignorant of his devices.

3. WHAT IS THE TRANSMIGRATION OF SOULS?

A. Transmigration is another word for reincarnation. It means the movement of life from one time-period and life species to another.

B. For example: in India, the word avatar means the incarnation of any god into a living human person. In its highest religious evaluation, avatar is the incarnation of Vishnu, a prominent Hindu god.

Some teachers of Hinduism believe that Vishnu has been reincarnated numerous times. Other Hindus teach that Vishnu has come as avatar nine times: as a fish, a tortoise, a man-lion, a boar, a child dwarf, Rama, Khristna, Buddha and Christ.

One can easily determine that this is a form of demon possession and that they are lying demon spirits and not a person living from other generations.

4. REINCARNATION

According to the National Enquirer, the soul in eternity who wins the assignment to a certain person then hovers near the parents for some time to make sure that he is willing to enter into that physical body. When the time is right and the physical blossoming occurs, he enters that newborn body, usually at the time of ejection but occasionally shortly before or after. If he hesitates too long, the baby will not live.

In the case of a stillborn baby, the body was not perfected, and a soul does not enter it. He will then have to start seeking again for a proper vehicle or wait his turn for those particular parents, if he was intent on living with them.

Surprisingly, there are almost as many candidates for deformed bodies of newborn babies as for the healthy, normal ones. This is an important lesson which we learn here: the greater the obstacles in the physical body, the more opportunity for a soul to pay off some past debts and achieve more rapid spiritual growth.

5. **WHO WERE THE FIRST HUMAN BEINGS TO BELIEVE IN REINCARNATION?**

A. The doctrine of metempsychosis means to put a soul into life, the supposed passing of the soul at death into another body, either human or animal by transmigration.

B. The belief in transmigration of human souls began in pagan lands where they submitted to demon power and refused to follow God.

God speaks to us through the book of Romans:

Romans 1:18-20,23,25, *For the wrath of god is revealed from heaven against all ungodliness and unrighteousness of men, who hold the truth in unrighteousness.*

v. 19, *Because that which may be known of God is manifest in them; for God hath shewed it unto them.*

v. 20, *For the invisible things of him from the creation of the world are clearly seen, being understood by the things that are made, even his eternal power and Godhead; so that they are without excuse:*

v. 23, *And changed the glory of the uncorruptible God into an image made like to corruptible man, and to birds, and fourfooted beasts, and creeping things.*

v. 25, *Who changed the truth of God into a lie, and worshipped and served the creature more than the Creator, who is blessed for ever. Amen.*

It was countries like India and Tibet which were the leaders in teaching the mystery of reincarnation.

C. Hinduism teaches various levels of consciousness.

   1) Higher consciousness is the road to nirvana.
   2) Unity consciousness seeks to bring a mystical union with the universe.

   3) God consciousness is when a Hindu considers himself actually God.

Such states of consciousness are experienced through hypnosis, mediumistic trance, certain drugs and witchcraft.

6. WHO TEACHES THE DOCTRINE OF REINCARNATION?

A. GURU: Literally means a teacher. Hinduism cannot be learned by reading, but must be taught by a guru who has been taught by a guru. Every Hindu must follow a guru. Every Hindu must follow a guru to reach self-realization.

B. It is through these gurus that tradition is passed from generation to generation.

C. The guru is worshipped through his life and after his death. Many Hindus believe that they can communicate with the guru more strongly after death. The grave of a guru is considered an ideal place for meditation.

7. WHAT SPECIFICALLY DOES REINCARNATION TEACH?

A. Reincarnation says the unattached soul seeking reality into a physical body can have a preference. He must clear it with a high authority.

B. Reincarnation is a doctrine of works of self-effort.

C. Reincarnation reaches the achievement of the final state of heaven without the need of God.

D. Reincarnation denies the birth, the death, the resurrection of Jesus Christ. It denies an atonement for sin.

E. The Bible teaches that:

1) Man is a sinner.

Romans 5:12, *Wherefore, as by one man sin entered into the world, and death by sin; and so death passed upon all men, for that all have sinned.*

2) He is lost without God.

Mark 16:16, *He that believeth and is baptized shall be saved; but he that believeth not shall be damned.*

3) Man can only be saved by Jesus Christ.

John 3:16, *For God so loved the world, that he gave his only begotten Son, that whosoever believeth in him should not perish, but have everlasting life.*

4) Man must face the judgment.

Hebrews 9:27, *And as it is appointed unto men once to die, but after this the judgment:*

8. WHAT IS THE BIBLICAL RELATIONSHIP TO THIS DOCTRINE?

A. God said in Hebrews 9:27, . . .*it is appointed unto men once to die. . .*

B. The rich man died and lifted up his eyes in hell.

Luke 16:23, *And in hell he lift up his eyes, being in torments, and seeth Abraham afar off, and Lazarus in his bosom.*

1) His memory was alert.

Luke 16:25, *But Abraham said, Son, remember that thou in thy lifetime receivedst thy good things, and likewise Lazarus evil things: but now he is comforted, and thou art tormented.*

2) His senses of feeling were strong.

Luke 16:24, *And he cried and said, Father Abraham, have mercy on me, and send Lazarus, that he may dip the tip of his finger in water, and cool my tongue; for I am tormented in this flame.*

3) His brothers were still living.

Luke 16:28, *For I have five brethren; that he may testify unto them, lest they also come into this place of torment.*

4) He was there to stay forever.

Luke 16:26, *And beside all this, between us and you there is a great gulf fixed: so that they which would pass from hence to you cannot; neither can they pass to us, that would come from thence.*

9. HOW DOES ONE GET INTO THE DOCTRINE?

A. Oriental Meditation

1) T.M. and Zen seek to project a person from rational thought into a higher state of consciousness.

2) These could be the paths of nothingness, the surrender to cosmic forces.

B. Yoga

Is literally "yoking" or union with Brahma. The ultimate goal is union with the Absolute.

1) Yoga teaches breath control and disciplining oneself to denounce all desires. It seeks to induce a state of trance or be removed from reality.

2) A yogi is one who has attained proficiency in yoga. The true yogi cuts himself off from all sense perceptions including his family, friends, and human relationships. He lives beyond space and time.

C. Reincarnation beyond controversy is:

1) A deceiving and false hope.

2) A debasing of human dignity.

3) A fatal lie to destroy the eternity of its followers.

INDIANA CHRISTIAN UNIVERSITY

DEMONOLOGY & DELIVERANCE II
PRINCIPALITIES & POWERS

Lesson 8

ARE THERE MONSTERS IN THE SPIRIT WORLD?

READING:

Revelation 16:12-14, *And the sixth angel poured out his vial upon the great river Euphrates; and the water thereof was dried up, that the way of the kings of the east might be prepared.*

v. 13, *And I saw three unclean spirits like frogs come out of the mouth of the dragon, and out of the mouth of the beast, and out of the mouth of the false prophet.*

v. 14, *For they are the spirits of devils, working miracles, which go forth unto the kings of the earth and of the whole world, to gather them to the battle of that great day of God Almighty.*

INTRODUCTION:

There are monsters in the spirit world. Is a person wrong in exposing Satan's work?

  A. Some people feel that exposing the works of Satan could be a form of exalting him.

  B. I feel that God is the greatest exposer of evil and that He says more about the devil than any other person!

  C. We must know and understand the principalities and powers of the spirit world.

  D. We must know the true story of how devils became devils and the end of all demon worship. We must know the judgments coming to the nether world spirits.

1. MONSTERS IN THE SPIRIT WORLD

  A. I have visited many heathen and pagan temples. Some are primitive, some are ornate. Some of their gods are monstrous in size and in looks.

They are oftentimes part-animal and part-human. The people are taught to worship these monsters of demon origin.

B. One of the monsters of the spirit world is the dragon. The Imperial Throne of China was called the Dragon Throne. I have seen it in the Forbidden City in Peking, China. The entire throne is a network of dragon heads and bodies.

The Chinese celebrate the year of the Dragon recurring every thirteen years.

C. Many people testify that in their experiences in temple worship they see serpents the size of dragons.

2. SNAKE WORSHIP

A. In some primitive countries as Dohomony in Africa, now called Benin, certain tribes have regular snake worship.
Every house has its own serpent. The people feed and prepare a nest for this snake. If a cart or bus happens to hit a snake, the people burn the house of the person who did it. He has killed a god!

B. Many of these serpents are poisonous. If one of these snakes bites its owner and he dies, the people say the gods were against him!

C. T.L. Osborn told me that his wife went to Dohomony to set up a meeting. At a nearby serpent temple, a priest had a huge snake around his head and body. He told Daisy, "This is our god!" She demanded, "Give me that snake." She took the snake from his hands and it instantly became as straight as a pole as if petrified. She turned to a trembling native preacher who was with her and said, "Take it!" He obeyed. The snake was still like a pole. She took it back and handed it to the priest and immediately the serpent went almost wild with struggling as it wrapped itself around the priest. Daisy said, "My God made all creation and we are not afraid of your snake god."

D. This reminds us of how Aaron threw his staff down before the magicians of Egypt to prove to them that "I Am" is God.

Exodus 7:10-12, *And Moses and Aaron went in unto Pharaoh, and they did so as the LORD had commanded: and Aaron cast down his rod before Pharaoh, and before his servants, and it became a serpent.*

v. 11, *Then Pharaoh also called the wisemen and the sorcerers: now the magicians of Egypt, they also did in like manner with their enchantments.*

v. 12, *For they cast down every man his rod, and they became serpents: but Aaron's rod swallowed up their rods.*

3. POLTERGEISTS OF THE SPIRIT WORLD

I have a clipping telling of parents who sent away their eight-year-old son because the poltergeist overturned their furniture and smashed their dishes. Mr. and Mrs. Charles Burden consulted a medium and were told their retarded son attracted spirits to their house. The medium said that poltergeists especially hurt retarded children who have no resistance. Mrs. Burden said that dishes were flying all over the house and her television set was overturned. A heater actually flew across the room. She called the police, who witnessed this and had no explanation. A spirit medium was called. He told the family to move out of the house.

The newspaper reported Mr. burden as saying, "I never believed in ghosts before, but I am convinced that there is a rotten spirit, a vile spirit, here. We have no dishes left whatsoever."

4. THE MOSLEMS' JINN

A. Moslems teach of spirit creatures they believe to be the watchmen of hell. Moslems believe the jinn are both male and female and they were created from fire. The Moslems believe that the jinny is a supernatural being that can take on human or animal forms. They believe the jinny can influence human affairs.

B. Sometimes drugs make these manifestations visible to humans.

C. Sometimes the delirium tremors of alcohol make the terrible creatures visible.

D. Many people living in insane asylums have seen into the spirit world, and witnessed horrifying creatures.

5. HAVE I SEEN A MONSTER?

A. Many times the devil has said to me, "Let me manifest myself." I have repeatedly said, "No, I will not accept any manifestation from the devil."

B. The devil cannot manifest himself unless you are a slave to serve him or he receives permission from you to do it.

C. I prayed for an attorney in Florida and he saw many very ugly faces crowding around him in a very menacing manner as I was setting him free.

D. Clarita Villaneueva saw a spirit demon. She said he looked ten feet high, had fangs and was very frightening to behold.

6. A BRAZILIAN WITCH DOCTOR EXPLAINS THE SPIRIT WORLD

A. Arlindo D. Olivera was a prominent witch doctor in Brazil, whom I took across America. We traveled from Florida to the state of Washington. I had Arlindo speak in meetings with me in places like Carnegie Hall in New York City and Constitution Hall in Washington, D.C.

B. Arlindo worked for the Brazilian government for many years, in the office of the Ministry of War, in the office of the President, and also in the office of an attorney.

C. Arlindo was dedicated to the devil before he was born. His mother went to a very strong witch doctor and she felt spirits enter her womb into her unborn baby. She said that she heard the demons say he was "their son."

D. When Arlindo was three years old the demons within him caused him to have strong seizures throwing him to the ground. They caused him to be unruly, making his parents almost hate him.

E. At this time a spirit who claimed to be Dr. Reubenstein, a German physician now deceased, manifested itself. This spirit in the three-year-old child would consult with people about their illnesses and write prescriptions in Latin with Arlindo's hand. The sick people took these prescriptions to the drug store and they were filled by the pharmacist. At this time Arlindo could not write Portuguese or Latin.

F. Arlindo said that at three years old, a few spirits manifested in him, but later there were at least 300 which he knew by name and which manifested themselves.

7. ARLINDO WAS REMOVED FROM HIS PARENTS WHEN THREE YEARS OLD

A. "When I was three years old, the spirits came upon me. They were endangering my health. My parents consulted an old African witch doctor. He said, 'the child must be taken to Africa for an apprenticeship where the resources and necessities (such as roots, herbs, etc.) for witchcraft are available.'

"The witch doctor promised to support me. He said my powers were already greater than his, and he had practiced for 60 years."

B. "My parents refused to permit the African witch doctor to take me to Africa. They were afraid they would never again see me.

But it was agreed that I be taken from my parents and live with my aunt who was a very fat woman and a spiritist."

C. Arlindo remembers that the African witch doctor was 84 years old, and had three tribal marks on his face. This witch doctor used the Epah (sea shells) to hear spirits, and wore a lion skin to receive messages from the spirits.

8. ARLINDO BECAME A TROUBLEMAKER

A. "The devils spoiled my life. I never had a normal childhood. Because of the devil in me, I never knew the love of a mother or father. When I went to school the spirits would make trouble. They would not let me study. They caused me to fight with the teacher. When the teacher would give me work to do, the spirit would give the answer before the teacher was through presenting the problem. This would make her very angry. The spirit in me would tell her that I knew more than she did."

B. "One day, when I was just eight years old, a spirit manifested itself in me while in school and I began to argue with the teacher. The spirit said, 'You are the teacher, but I know more than you do.' The teacher complained to the principal, and I was discharged from school."

9. ARLINDO AND HIS FATHER

A. "At 16, the spirits manifested strongly. I would faint on the streets. I was picked up and taken by ambulance to the hospital or to jail. At this time, I was living with my parents."

B. "One night a spirit manifested in me and I did not come home until 2 a.m. My father met me and said, 'What kind of a time in the night is this to come home?' The spirit replied to my father, 'It's no business of yours.' This angered my father and he spoke bitterly to me. The spirit argued back. My father got a piece of wood to strike me. The spirit said, 'If you are a man, you can hit me with that.' But my father's arm became frozen upraised, and he could not bring it down. 'Who are you?' my father asked. The spirit responded, 'I am Summa Quis Summa Qua. I lived long before you.' My father could not believe it until the spirit told how he was the spirit who gave the enchantment which made it possible for my father to get my mother to marry him. She did not want to do so.

My father broke down and confessed that the spirit was right and that he now believed in the spirit."

C. "After that my father supported me and my spirit work. Summa Quis Summa Qua said that he was originally an African who had died at the age of 165. Also, he had lived in 350 persons previous to that."

10. ARLINDO, WERE YOU ABOVE THE WITCH DOCTOR?

A. "Did you belong to a group or sect of witch doctors?"

"Yes, I was head of Congere (con-jay-ray). Our sect was prohibited by the police of Rio de Janiero. We were not registered as a lawful sect."

B. "I had 300 different spirits in me who would not permit me to try to register with the authorities. They said they were greater authorities than the human authorities and warned that if I tried to register they would permit me to get caught and punished. If I refused to register, they promised to protect me and they did, for I was never caught by the police and punished."

11. ARLINDO, DID YOU HAVE A CHIEF SPIRIT POSSESSING YOU?

A. "Yes, Ta Ta Caveira (Father Skull Bones or Father Skeleton) was my chief spirit. He said he had always existed and had never reincarnated and that he was not the spirit of a dead man. He said he was on the earth from the beginning and was already tired of being here when Jesus came. He was one of the cemetery spirits and claimed to have 7,771 spirits in his legion. He looked like a large, strong, fine looking white man with glasses, reddish blonde hair, and wore a business suit. When he manifested to me he looked like a skeleton."

B. "This spirit liked to attend funerals. I would see him sitting on top of the coffin. He liked to drink rum, so I always kept about eight quarts of rum and four quarts of wine in my house for Tata."

C. "Tata would require me to cut myself and offer my blood."

12. I ASKED ARLINDO WHICH SPIRITS MANIFESTED IN HIM MOST OFTEN?

A. "Oxala (Oh-chal-ah), the head of all spirits."

B. "Oxun (Oh-chun), the Virgin Mary."

C. "Obum (Oh-boom), known as St. George."

D. "Oxafun (Oh Chal-ah-foon), also called the Holy Spirit."

E. "Oxaci (Oh-schassi), prayed to as St. Sebastian."

F. "Abaliuet (Ah-bal-ee-you-ay), St Lazarus. He is king of the cemeteries.

When he manifested, he would twist my body so terribly that my assistants would have to pour oil on my limbs and work with them to straighten out the contorted joints. Abaliuet made me eat meat which had been left in the sun until it was rotten. I washed it down my throat with olive oil."

13. THE KING OF ALL DEVILS

I asked Arlindo, who was the king of all the demons he knew. Arlindo said, "All the witchcraft sects consider Oxala the head of all spirits.

His African name of Oxala (Oh-schal-lah) is equal to the claims of Jesus Christ."

14. CAPTAIN CRAZY

A. Arlindo said, "One of my spirits was called Captain Crazy or Captain Insane. He is actually the intellectual type of spirit. He speaks Portuguese, Spanish, French, English, German, etc. He discusses science, engineering, law, etc. He can reveal secrets of international events, politics, etc."

B. "When he manifests, I lie down on a bed and go into a trance. Then he consults politicians and military and legal people. He would say, 'Attention, there is a cabinet meeting now being held in the White House in Washington, etc.' The next day the news of this would be carried in the newspapers."

15. ARLINDO, DID ALL THE DEMONS YOU PERSONALLY KNEW HAVE NAMES?

A. "Yes, all the demons had names. I have had manifested at one time or another in me at least 300 spirits. Some of the spirits were leaders of groups, or commanders of legions."

B. "One named Ta Ta Caveria (translated Father of Skull Bones or Father Skeleton) claimed to have 7,771 spirits in his legion. Another spirit was feminine in type and was called Emaja, The Queen of the Sea."

C. "I have personally seen thousands of demons at a time, rising like a cloud of birds. From what I have learned, there are millions of demons in the spirit world. Many claim to be dead saints, the same as the images of the Roman Catholic Church."

D. "Perhaps I can tell you how many devils there are if you can tell me how many ants there are in all the anthills of the world. There are millions of them. Clouds of them"

   E. "Xato Boroko Tjembo said there were 10,000 demons in his legion."

16. ARLINDO, WHERE DID ALL THESE DEMONS COME FROM TO POSSESS PEOPLE IN BRAZIL?

   A. "The devils claimed to come from different places. One said he was from Canada—an Indian spirit. Most of the ones that I knew came from Africa."

   B. "Some claimed that they came from India."

   C. "One told me he had come from the moon."

   D. "Another spirit told me he was from the sun."

   E. "Some devils claim to be the spirits of departed dead people. They take pride in telling their names, where they had lived, and what they did in persons. They would describe their homes and details of their lives to me. They often told how the person died. One spirit claimed to be a Dr. Rubenstein. He manifested in me when I was three years old and would write prescriptions for sick people."

   F. "One of my spirits claimed to be a 32nd Mason."

   G. "Now, however, I believe these were lying demons."

17. DID ANY OF THE SPIRITS WHICH MANIFESTED IN YOU LOOK LIKE ANIMALS?

   A. "Yes, there was a spirit named, Ta, Ta, Veludu which means Father Velvet. He looked like an ape, very dark and hairy. He also talked like an ape. Father Velvet would guard my yard and my sessions from the police."

   B. "He would put rum into a calabash shell and make me drink it. Veldu spoke very coarsely and harshly. When he was on guard for me, he would whistle when the police were coming. Then I would make a special enchantment and the police would become confused and fail to find me. Ta Ta Veludu claimed to have always existed and was not the spirit of a man once on earth. Others looked like Veludu, some had human heads and beast bodies."

18. ARLINDO, DID YOU LOVE THE DEMON SPIRITS AND DID THEY LOVE YOU?

    A. "No, I actually hated some of them."

    B. "The devils call their mediums 'apparatus,' using them like a tool or a machine. Some devils called me, 'my donkey.' They have no respect for their mediums as human beings, but often speak contemptuously of them and use them like pieces of machinery."

    C. "The term 'apparatus' is no more to the spirit than a radio is to a human—a sender or a receiver of messages. The medium is just an apparatus."

19. ARLINDO, DID THESE SPIRITS STAY IN YOU OR COME OCCASIONALLY?

"The demon spirits would always advance toward me, face on. The devils always retire facing me. I have never seen a devil turn his back on anyone. Sometimes they would just melt into a wall. Sometimes they would go up like a whirlwind. Other times they would vanish like a light being turned off. When the spirits came, it always caused an uncomfortable feeling in me. I would have a hot flash or a chill, or the hair on my head would stand on end. Also, I sometimes felt dizzy. At times, I felt ill by a pain in my stomach. Other times, my eyes filmed over. I never felt good when they came."

20. ARLINDO, HOW COULD YOU TELL IT WAS A SPIRIT MATERIALIZING BEFORE YOU?

    A. "The spirits were sometimes able to materialize fully so I could not tell whether they were human or spirit. I could tell by looking at their feet, for the spirit's feet never touch the ground. They walk as on feet, and they make noise as though their shoes are on the ground, but they stay about a palm's width above the ground."

    B. "Sometimes the spirits don't materialize as humans but come in appearance of animals, like cats, or apes, or grotesque with animal heads, or several heads or hands."

21. ARLINDO, DID YOU EVER MEET SATAN, THE CHIEF OF ALL DEMONS?

    A. "Yes, but at the time I did not know he was the head of the demons. He was called Eixu (Esch-you)."

    B. "When he manifested, I sang Lucifer's Hymn. Some of the words were:
        He is the king of Hell
        He has two heads

> One is the king of hell
> The other is Jesus of Nazareth
> One works for good, and one works for bad.

C. "Eixu likes to be praised. We would tell him, 'You are the greatest!' He seemed have millions of demons in his control, but my chief spirit Ta Ta Caveira never paid him any particular attention or honor."

D. "Also there is a 'female' spirit called the devil's wife. (Though there is no real sex in the spirits, they take on a male or female form.)"

E. "This female devil is called Bomba Gira and when she appears, she is always at the side of Eixu. She also has seven devils who are her husbands. She is the protector of prostitutes. She helps prostitutes get business."

22. ARLINDO, DID DEMONS EVER HURT YOU PHYSICALLY?

A. "Sometimes the spirits made me cut myself, then collect the blood, mix it with wine, and make the person asking aid of me to drink the mixture, as part of the enchantment to secure their desired satisfaction."

B. "I didn't feel any pain when I cut myself with a dagger. The spirits would have me put chalk on the wound to stop the blood, and soon I would heal up."

C. "Many times I was hurt or cut by the spirits. This was 'sacrificing my blood,' so some of my clients could be helped. Also, they did it because they liked to drink my blood. After cutting my arm or leg, I would suck the blood and let the spirit enjoy it. Once I found a dagger sticking through the calf of my leg. I pulled it out without pain and it healed up quickly."

23. ARLINDO, DID THE DEMONS HURT YOUR FAMILY?

A. "Yes, my family is mostly sad."

B. "Emaja, Queen of the Sea, and Abaliuet, the Head of the Cemetery (Lazarus), both liked my brother. When the child was about eight years old they both claimed him as 'my son.' My family had a spiritualist session and gave an offering to Emaja, casting it on the sea to appease her and get her to surrender the body. This she refused to do. The witch doctor tried to appease the spirit of Lazarus, making a gift in the cemetery. He refused to surrender. As a result, they killed my brother. We were in the room during the final struggle of two powerful demons."

24. ARLINDO'S CONVERSION

"Before my conversion to Jesus Christ, I thought I was serving God and I was very proud of myself. When these spirits drove my wife and family away from our home, I had to take refuge in the home of my sister who was saved. A minister who lived next door had compassion on me and drove the devils out forever."

CONCLUSION:

This is the world of evil spirits—just beyond the human eye.

NOTES

INDIANA CHRISTIAN UNIVERSITY

DEMONOLOGY & DELIVERANCE II
PRINCIPALITIES & POWERS

Lesson 9

ARE CURSES REAL?

READING:

Genesis 3:14, . . .*Because thou hast done this, thou art cursed. . .*

INTRODUCTION:

Curses are very old on planet earth.

1. WHAT IS A CURSE?

Curse, according to Webster's Dictionary, means: "To call down wrath upon someone - a calling on God or the gods to send evil or injury down on some person or thing."

2. THE DEVIL WAS THE FIRST TO BE CURSED

Genesis 3:13-15, *And the Lord God said unto the woman, What is this that thou hast done? And the woman said, The serpent beguiled me, and I did eat.*

v. 14, *And the LORD God said unto the serpent, Because thou hast done this, thou art cursed above all cattle, and above every beast of the field; upon thy belly shalt thou go, and dust shalt thou eat all the days of thy life:*

v. 15, *And I will put enmity between thee and the woman, and between thy seed and her seed; it shall bruise thy head, and thou shalt bruise his heal.*

3. GOD SENT CURSES UPON HIS CREATION BECAUSE OF REBELLION AGAINST HIM

Genesis 3:17-19, *And unto Adam he said, Because thou hast hearkened unto the voice of thy wife, and hast eaten of the tree, of which I commanded thee, saying, thou shalt not eat of it: cursed is the ground for thy sake; in sorrow shalt thou eat of it all the days of thy life;*

v. 18, *Thorns also and thistles shall it bring forth to thee; and thou shalt eat the herb of the field.*

v. 19, *In the sweat of thy face shalt thou eat bread, till thou return unto the ground; for out of it wast thou taken: for dust thou art, and unto dust shalt thou return.*

4. CAIN WAS CURSED BECAUSE OF MURDER

Genesis 4:10-12, *And he said, What hast thou done? the voice of thy brother's blood crieth unto me from the ground.*

v. 11, *And now art thou cursed from the earth, which hath opened her mouth to receive thy brother's blood from thy hand;*

v. 12, *When thou tillest the ground, it shall not henceforth yield unto thee her strength; a fugitive and a vagabond shalt thou be in the earth.*

5. THE DEVIL CURSED BECAUSE OF MURDER

A. He especially wants to curse those who are militant for Jesus.

B. Of late years, many people have come to me believing they were living under the burden of a curse. Some believe the curse had followed their families for generations.

6. BALAAM WAS PAID TO CURSE ISRAEL

Numbers 23:1, 6-11, 23, *And Balaam said unto Balak, Build me here seven altars, and prepare me here seven oxen and seven rams.*

v. 6, *And he returned unto him, and, lo, he stood by his burnt sacrifice, he, and all the princes of Moab.*

v. 7, *And he took up his parable, and said, Balak the king of Moab hath brought me from Aram, out of the mountains of the east, saying, Come, curse me Jacob, and come, defy Israel.*

v. 8, *How shall I curse, whom God hath not cursed? or how shall I defy, whom the LORD hath not defied?*

v. 9, *For from the top of the rocks I see him, and from the hills I behold him: lo, the people shall dwell alone, and shall not be reckoned among the nations.*

v. 10, *Who can count the dust of Jacob, and the number of the fourth part of Israel? Let me die the death of the righteous, and let my last end be like his!*

v. 11, *And Balak said unto Balaam, What hast thou done unto me? I took thee to curse mine enemies, and, behold, thou hast blessed them altogether.*

v. 23, Surely there is no enchantment against Jacob, neither is there any divination against Israel: according to this time it shall be said of Jacob and of Israel, What hath God wrought!

This is one of the greatest truths of all time. The devil is unable to curse God's people who are covered by His love and power.

7. REUBEN WAS CURSED BY HIS FATHER

Reuben was cursed because of adultery.

Genesis 49:3-4, Reuben, thou art my first born, my might, and the beginning of my strength, the excellency of dignity, and the excellency of power:

v. 4, Unstable as water, thou shalt not excel; because thou wentest up to thy father's bed; then defiledst thou it: he went up to my couch.

Genesis 35:22, And it came to pass, when Israel dwelt in that land, that Reuben went and lay with Bilhah his father's concubine: and Israel heard it...

8. DO NOT BRING CURSED THINGS BEFORE GOD

Deuteronomy 7:26, Neither shalt thou bring an abomination into thine house, lest thou be a cursed thing like it: but thou shalt utterly detest it, and thou shalt utterly abhor it; for it is a cursed thing.

9. WITCHCRAFT CURSES OR HEXES

A. It is believed that a curse can last 1,000 years, from generation to generation.

B. Nations have been cursed.

C. Cain, the first person to bear a curse, was a murderer.

D. Archaeologists have unearthed in Greece a lead tablet, possibly 2,300 years old, engraved with a curse: "I curse the head DIODORUS, and turn away from Arternidora his face, his ears, his body. . .I curse their love and turn it to hate."

10. CAN CHRISTIANS BE CURSED?

A. Balaam said in Numbers 23:8, *How shall I curse, whom God hath not cursed?*

B. Jesus said in Mark 16:18, *They shall take up serpents; and if they drink any deadly thing, it shall not hurt them; they shall lay hands on the sick, and they shall recover.*

Luke 10:19, *Behold, I give unto you power to tread on serpents and scorpions, and over all the power of the enemy: and nothing shall by any means hurt you.*

His disciples went into the wilderness of demon activity.

C. Paul found it in every city.

Acts 16:16, *And it came to pass, as we went to prayer, a certain damsel possessed with a spirit of divination met us, which brought her masters much gain by soothsaying.*

D. James 4:6, *But he giveth more grace. wherefore he saith, God resisteth the proud, but giveth grace unto the humble.*

11. RETURN THE DEVIL'S CURSES DOUBLE

Revelation 18:6, *Reward her even as she rewarded you, and double unto her double according to her works: in the cup which she hath filled fill to her double.*

12. WHEN WILL CURSES END?

Revelation 22:3, *And there shall be no more curse: but the throne of God and of the Lamb shall be in it; and his servants shall serve him.*

INDIANA CHRISTIAN UNIVERSITY

DEMONOLOGY & DELIVERANCE II
PRINCIPALITIES & POWERS

Lesson 10

CAN WITCHES STOP WITCHES?

READING:

Luke 11:17-23, *But he, knowing their thoughts, said unto them, Every kingdom divided against itself is brought to desolation; and a house divided against a house falleth.*

v. 18, *If Satan also be divided against himself, how shall his kingdom stand? because ye say that I cast out devils through Beelzebub.*

v. 19, *And if I by Beelzebub cast out devils, by whom do your sons cast them out? therefore shall they be your judges.*

v. 20, *But if I with the finger of God cast out devils, no doubt the kingdom of god is come upon you.*

v. 21, *When a strong man armed keepeth his palace, his goods are in peace:*

v. 22, *But when a stronger than he shall come upon him, and overcome him, he taketh from him all his armour wherein he trusted, and divideth his spoils.*

v. 23, *He that is not with me is against me: and he that gathereth not with me scattereth.*

INTRODUCTION:

Witchcraft is greatly on the rise in America. Some cities claim thousands of witches are living there.

1. ARE WITCHES FOR REAL?

A. Does a belief in witches mean that you are naive and superstitious and not up-to-date with Western culture?

B. Are witches confined to primitive parts of the world, or are they found in Europe, England and America?

Geography, culture, and riches have nothing to do with witchcraft. The devil can deceive anyone who will give his mind over to him.

2. CAN WITCHES STOP WITCHES?

A. In the area of demon power, there are degrees and variations of power. These are not at all like the caricatures such as Bewitched, I Dream of Jeannie, The Six Million Dollar Man or Wonder Woman.

B. Ephesians 6:12, *For we wrestle not against flesh and blood, but against principalities, against powers, against the rulers of darkness of this world, against spiritual wickedness in high places.*

There are principalities of demon authority. A principality is an area where a prince rules over his subjects. This means that in the world of evil spirits there are categories of authority and areas which certain spirits rule.

C. There are evil spirits who command other evil spirits.

For example, Arlindo Barbosa, the Brazilian witch doctor, declares that two demons fought over possession of his brother. The battle was so great that the demon spirits killed his eight-year-old brother. Arlindo, the witch doctor, was in the room in a trance and saw the battle and the demons leave the room screaming and cursing as his brother lay dead on the bed.

D. Jesus Christ said in Matthew 12:43-45 that a certain man was cleansed of an evil spirit and that the spirit went into dry places and "seeking rest and findeth none" and returned to his former victim and found him:

1) Empty

2) Swept

3) Garnished

Jesus said that this demon had the opportunity to bring in seven other spirits more wicked than himself. This key spirit had power to direct seven other evil spirits and repossess that man.

Jesus declared the last end of that man to be worse than the first.

E. In my global experiences, I have often witnessed deep rivalry and hatred between demon spirits. There is boasting of who is greatest and most powerful. There is the bossing and governing by ruler spirits.

3. THE DICTIONARY SAYS:

A. A woman practicing the black arts is called a witch. Witches are said to be possessed by supernatural powers, by a pact made with the devil or a familiar spirit. The use of witchery is a deliberate and intentional interaction with the devil or a familiar spirit, which is a fantastic power of evil.

B. A warlock is a male witch. The two are usually together.

C. Some people think that a witch can transport herself through the air on a broom. Some believe a witch could turn into an animal. Many were afraid of the spell or curse of the witches.

4. THE WITCHES AND THE SORCERER

A. The same original words can be translated, "sorcerer" or "witch." It is the pretended divination of the unknown in connection with demon powers and idol worship.

B. This art, in ancient times, was also practiced in connection with pharmacology or the mixing of drugs into medical compounds for various healings.

5. WITCHES EMBRACE VARIOUS FORMS OF PAGANISM

Historically, their religion is a worship of Satan through an ancient horned god.

6. WIZARD

A. A term denoting a person pretending to be wise regarding unknown factors, but the term is usually employed as the masculine of witch or warlock.

B. There are many variations of witchcraft practiced today; however, they all hold essentially the same beliefs and practices.

7. THE BIBLE VERY CAREFULLY DEALS WITH THE REALITY OF WITCHCRAFT

A. Exodus 22:18, *Thou shalt not suffer a witch to live.*

B. Deuteronomy 18:10, *There shall not be found among you any one that maketh his son or his daughter to pass through the fire, or that useth divination, or an observer of times, or an enchanter, or a witch.*

C. The sad end of King Saul, the first king of Israel, is recorded in I Samuel 15:23, *For rebellion is as the sin of witchcraft, and stubbornness is as iniquity and idolatry. Because thou hast rejected the word of the LORD, he hath also rejected thee from being king.* King Saul went from stubbornness and rebellion to a witch at En-dor.

I Samuel 28:7, *Then said Saul unto his servants, Seek me a woman that hath a familiar spirit, that I may go to her, and inquire of her. And his servants said to him, Behold, there is a woman that hath a familiar spirit at En-dor.*

D. God spoke to a nation in II Kings 9:22, *And it came to pass, when Joram saw Jehu, that he said, Is it peace, Jehu? And he answered, What peace, so long as the whoredoms of thy mother Jezebel and her witchcrafts are so many?*

E. A king who had an ancestry like Moses and David turned to witchcraft.

II Chronicles 33:6, *And he caused his children to pass through the fire in the valley of the son of Hinnom: also he observed times, and used enchantments, and used witchcraft, and dealt with a familiar spirit, and with wizards: he wrought much evil in the sight of the LORD, to provoke him to anger..*

F. God rebuked the nation of Israel.

Micah 5:12, *And I will cut off witchcrafts out of thine hand; and thou shalt have no more soothsayers.*

This reveals the anger of God against demon activities. It is so polluting and contagious that God demands a clean-up of the land.

G. The Prophet Nahum described the people of Nineveh.

Nahum 3:4, *Because of the multitude of the whoredoms of the well-favoured harlot, the mistress of witchcrafts, that selleth nations through her whoredoms, and families through her witchcrafts.*

H. The Apostle Paul described the works of the flesh.

Galatians 5:20, *Idolatry, witchcraft, hatred, variance, emulations, wrath, strife, seditions, heresies.*

I. Sorcery was practiced in Samaria.

Acts 8:9-11, *But there was a certain man, called Simon, which beforetime in the same city used sorcery, and bewitched the people of Samaria, giving out that himself was some great one:*

v. 10, *To whom they all gave heed, from the least to the greatest, saying, this man is the great power of God.*

v. 11, *And to him they had regard, because that of long time he had bewitched them with sorceries.*

J. God says that judgment will not change men from worshipping devils.

Revelation 9:21, *Neither repented they of their murders, nor of their sorceries, nor of their fornication, nor of their thefts.*

There is no true love or goodwill among demons. They are full of division, and cause humans to be likewise.

There is a proliferation of witchcraft. Some more powerful witches can stop other less powerful witches. There is a constant war over who controls and possesses the most power.

NOTES

INDIANA CHRISTIAN UNIVERSITY

DEMONOLOGY & DELIVERANCE II
PRINCIPALITIES & POWERS

Lesson 11

HAUNTED HOUSES AND GHOSTS

READING:

Joshua 6:18, *And ye, in any wise keep yourselves from the accursed thing, lest ye make yourselves accursed, when ye take of the accursed thing, and make the camp of Israel a curse, and trouble it.*

INTRODUCTION:

Houses are built to be dwelling places for human families.

Just as a human person has a personality, so a house can possess a personality. This personality is formed by what takes place in the home.

1. GOD'S HOUSE

In God's house, the temple in Jerusalem, the living Spirit of the eternal Elohim was manifested over the golden cherubim revealing God's presence and acceptance of their worship. This dwelling place of supreme deity was the holy of holies. It was a true house of God.

2. HEATHEN TEMPLES

Just as the house of worship of the true God has a particular spirit in it, so houses of demon worship are dwelling places of demon entities.

Also, houses where families reside can become demon inhabited.

3. THE SWISS CASTLE

I was a guest in an ancient castle in Switzerland. My bedroom was upstairs in a turret or tower. I had to take a lighted lamp with me to see the way, as there were no electric lights on the stairs or in the bedroom. The doors screeched; the windows were long and narrow.

The furniture was ancient. The pictures on the wall were almost frightening.

Our host was a lady in her seventies or eighties. She had told the history of her family and the castle before we retired that evening.

It took great courage to go into that room. It took more courage to stay in there. My flesh moved and it seemed that I was not alone. There are houses which have known tragedy and human hurt and have become dwelling places of demons.

4. A MAN WITH SEVEN DEVILS IN JAVA, INDONESIA

A. In Java, Howard Carter and I stayed with a family where the man of the house had seven demons manifested in him. These spirits would not permit his wife to sleep in the same bed with him. The demons would pinch her body and throw her onto the floor at night.

B. The wife showed Howard Carter and me the "holy cabinet" or altar. Inside the secret altar, the possessed man had a silver dagger which hung by a silver thread. Before, it had been a candleholder and a place where incense was burned. When the man knelt before the dagger and prayed while burning the incense, it caused the demons to manifest.

C. The husband knew the spirits by name. He commanded the spirits to do various things for him, including causing an enemy to die. The man owned a banana plantation and was an official at the railroad company. He was not a fool or a social misfit.

D. In that house, Mr. Carter and I, in our bedroom, were disturbed in the night. An entity stood at the foot of our bed and called Rev. Carter by his given name of Howard, asking what he was doing in that house. We both were awakened and began to plead the blood of Jesus over the demon spirit, commanding it to go. It left the room, but not our memory.

5. THE HOUSE IN MISHAWAKA, INDIANA

Spirit manifestation is not geographical.

Our local newspaper carried a bizarre story of a family having stones and bricks thrown at their house. The stones were on the ground and the concussion marks on the wall, but no person could be found. Then their refrigerator began to shift about the room by its own power. The television set moved around. They would come home from work to a house of overturned furniture and a very distressing atmosphere. They called the local police and officers saw the disarray.

The family finally came to me for exorcism. I prayed for them, and the manifestations ceased.

6. TWO DAUGHTERS DIED

A. Haunted houses can be dangerous. A friend of Rev. Howard of London, England lost two daughters in a haunted house.

The family moved into an older house. They had three teenage daughters.

One, who slept in a certain room, complained of being awakened and tormented at night by spirits. The parents, being Christians, refused to listen and told her the newness of their living in the place caused her fear. The disturbance grew worse. the parents still would not listen. This daughter died rather mysteriously.

B. Her sister was given that room. She immediately made the same complaints to her father. She said, "I am terrified of the room where my sister died." Her parents felt she was superstitious. A few months later she mysteriously died. The parents panicked. They only had one child left. They called for their pastor to pray in the room. He did, and there were such strong manifestations that he recommended they move out of the house. The demon activity was the reason it was standing empty.

7. HAUNTED HOUSES

A haunted house is a house in which supernatural spirits reside and manifest themselves. The manifestations of demons in a house usually are the result of the practice of witchcraft, or some terrible crime such as a murder having taken place there.

Demon entities use many different forms, including manifestations in all the five senses. The manifestation is usually to announce their presence or to annoy humans. These are related to the history of that house.

A. Sound—Haunted houses are often characterized by strong rappings, poundings, clanging, and footsteps late at night.

Human voices are common, both intelligible and unintelligible. Groans and moans are perhaps the most frequent. Animal sounds and inanimate sounds such as telephones ringing or music being played have been reported.

B. Sight—Appearances of shadowy figures of human-like beings, animals, or strange objects are considered traditional signs of haunted houses. Sometimes religious symbols, such as crucifixes and witchcraft emblems, appear.

C. Touch—Temperatures change in the body. Sometimes sudden drops in temperature and sudden rises in temperature occur in some haunted houses. Many people who have experienced spirit encounters in haunted houses have described their experience as strange, unholy feelings that covered their entire bodies.

D. Taste—Dr. Julies Reiter is perhaps the only person who has recorded tasting a ghost. He claims that he was physically assaulted by a ghost and, in the struggle, he bit his attacker as a last-ditch effort to be released. He described the taste as cold, rubbery, and lifeless.

E. Odor—"The smell of death" is a vivid way to describe the ghastly, musty, sickening odor that pervades some haunted houses.

F. Sometimes the spirits in haunted houses manifest themselves in tangible forms. The records of the Salem witch trials indicate that some of the victims of the hauntings in Salem left bruises, cuts, and bites inflicted on human bodies by the spirits.

G. Clarita Villenueva in Manila had bites and bruises on her body inflicted by a demon in the presence of medical doctors.

H. Throwing and moving of objects in haunted houses is common. Opening and closing of doors and windows, hurling of stones, books, and setting of fires characterizes haunted houses.

I. The Swanton Novers Rectory in England was haunted in 1919 with the particular manifestation of a mysterious dripping of water and oil from the ceiling. No physical explanation could be offered after repeated studies. Yet, it could not be denied that over fifty gallons of the mysterious substance was collected.

J. The Bible and other symbols of Christ's authority are sometimes attacked in haunted houses. In one case, a Bible was partially burned and the remaining portion was opened to an account in Mark's gospel about an exorcism.

K. In one haunted house, in 1851, the spirits collected clothes from all parts of the house and arranged them to depict a prayer meeting. Most of the figures had Bibles, each of which was opened to a chapter about demon spirits.

8. THE MOST HAUNTED HOUSE

The Borley Rectory in Essex House, England has been labeled as the most haunted house. In 1937-38, researchers into paranormal experiences investigated the house for fourteen months and logged over two thousand ghostly events. The most dramatic was the appearance of a nun asking for prayers and mass to deliver her tormented soul, and the appearance of a coach driven by a headless man.

9. A POPULARIZED HAUNTED HOUSE

A. A popularized haunted house in our times is the Long Island home publicized as the "Amityville Horror." A young family moved into what they thought was their "dream home," but turned out to be a nightmare. Red liquid flooded through the keyholes, green slime oozed from the walls, strange odors penetrated the atmosphere, the temperature shifted as much as fifteen degrees instantly, weird sounds like "an elephant rolling over in its sleep" and innumerable other ghostly experiences drove them out of their home after only 28 days. Major newspapers, magazines, television shows, a book, and a full-length movie have immortalized the demonic encounters in this haunting.

B. Haunted houses have existed since the earliest of times. Animist cultures still have their "taboo" houses where the spirits of the dead reside.

C. Ancient Egyptian, Roman, Greek and possibly every culture have recognized that certain houses and places were locations of special spirit activity.

10. WHAT THE BIBLE SAYS ABOUT HAUNTED HOUSES

A. The spirits which inhabit buildings are not the spirits of dead people. The Bible does not teach that dead people's spirits can return to haunt or communicate with the living. The only Biblical reference to such an occurrence is in I Samuel 28:12 when King Saul visited the witch of Endor. The witch screamed with horror when the spirit of one called Samuel came to the seance because she had never actually communicated with the dead before in her incantations.

B. The ghostly events in haunted houses can be explained as the work of demons. We have seen in this study that demons speak, throw victims around, and cause all sorts of manifestations even in the so-called haunted houses.

C. Just as the devil can possess a person, he can possess an object or a house. This is the reason Israel was commanded to totally destroy the cities of Canaan. They had been involved in demonic activity, and through idol worship had become accursed places.

Joshua 6:17-18, *And the city shall be accursed, even it, and all that are therein, to the LORD: only Rahab the harlot shall live, she and all that are with her in the house, because she hid the messengers that we sent.*

v. 18, *And ye, in any wise keep yourselves from the accursed thing, lest ye make yourselves accursed, when ye take of the accursed thing, and make the camp of Israel a curse, and trouble it.*

D. Haunted houses can be dealt with in two ways.

1) Destroy the place.

2) Deliver the place by prayer and dedicate the structure to the worship of God.

Joshua 6:24-25, *And they burnt the city with fire, and all that was therein: only the silver, and the gold, and the vessels of brass and of iron, they put into the treasury of the house of the LORD.*

v. 25, *And Joshua saved Rahab the harlot alive, and her father's household, and all that she had; and she dwelleth in Israel even unto this day; because she hid the messengers, which Joshua sent to spy out Jericho.*

INDIANA CHRISTIAN UNIVERSITY

DEMONOLOGY & DELIVERANCE II
PRINCIPALITIES & POWERS

Lesson 12

BLACK AND WHITE MAGIC

READING:

Deuteronomy 18:10, *There shall not be found among you any one that maketh his son or his daughter to pass through the fire, or that useth divination, or an observer of times, or an enchanter, or a witch,*

v. 11, *Or a charmer, or a consulter with familiar spirits, or a wizard, or a necromancer.*

INTRODUCTION:

The devil wishes to divide up his works in many fashions and under diverse names.

1. WHAT IS THE DIFFERENCE BETWEEN BLACK AND WHITE MAGIC?

A. The word magic is from the Hebrew word, *heret*. It means "to engrave." It has to do with drawing magical lines or circles.

B. White magic is presumed to only bless and help humanity. It does not become involved in hurting people or cursing them.

C. Black magic is presumed to be deadly medicine. It deals in all kinds of curses and angry demon activity.

D. Both black and white magic claim supernatural power from the spirit world. The difference is that black magic is always malevolent. It curses, kills, and destroys. It calls evil spirits into action against an enemy to destory or to hurt.

E. White magic claims to be a benevolent power which helps you find lost property or heals a sick person, or keeps back infernal powers which wish to destroy.

2. THE ART OF VOODOO

Voodoo claims to operate in both black and white magic, but under different names.

3. IS INCENSE BURNING POWERFUL?

A. All magic, whether black or white, practice incense burning of some sort.

B. In Brazil, the smoke of the cigar, while the witch is under the power of a spirit, makes the communication possible.

4. ARE FETISHES POWERFUL?

Both black and white magic use many kinds of religious paraphernalia to show their power. It can be a doll with pins stuck in it to curse an individual.

5. GOD'S VIEWPOINT

A. As far as God is concerned, all supernatural activity outside His divine operation is of a demonic source. It is our dependence on the devil for information that disturbs God. Satan demands worship from those through whom he manifests himself.

B. All magic claims the power of working wonders beyond the ordinary powers of man whether in a domestic or scientific operation.

C. Black and white magic make claims of supernatural power either by a celestial or infernal agency. Both systems of demonism have taken their origin in early human history. They have both sought to deal in miracles outside of God.

D. There are a multitude of accounts of the use of the nether world magic in the Old Testament. It is condemned by the prophets of God.

E. In the New Testament there are strong words regarding magic.

Acts 13:10, *And said, O full of all subtilty and all mischief, thou child of the devil, thou enemy of all righteousness, wilt thou not cease to pervert the right ways of the Lord?*

Galatians 5:20, *Idolatry, witchcraft, hatred, variance, emulations, wrath, strife, seditions, heresies.*

Philip, the deacon, found a famous magician in Samaria, known as Simon Magus, who while having great power with the people, is not said to have been able to work wonders (Acts 8:9-24).

6. THE BIBLE VERY DISTINCTLY PROHIBITS ALL MAGICAL ARTS

A. God condemns them.

Deuteronomy 18:10-11, *There shall not be found among you any one that maketh his son or his daughter to pass through the fire, or that useth divination, or an observer of times, or an enchanter, or a witch,*

v, 11, Or a charmer, or a consulter with familiar spirits, or a wizard, or a necromancer.

From this specification, it is evident that God has included every form of magical art as evil.

B. The Israelites were commanded not to practice witchcraft as it is the abomination of the people they found in the promised land.

NOTES

INDIANA CHRISTIAN UNIVERSITY

DEMONOLOGY & DELIVERANCE II
PRINCIPALITIES & POWERS

Lesson 13

WHAT IS CABALA?

READING:

I John 4:1, *Beloved, believe not every spirit, but try the spirits whether they are of God: because many false prophets are gone out into the world.*

INTRODUCTION:

There are sophisticated occult manifestations in the intellectual world. One of these is Cabala.

1. WHAT IS CABALA?

Cabala means, according to Webster's Dictionary:

   A. Cabal, French for intrigue, a plot, a tremendous influence.

   B. A small group with secret design or doctrines.

   C. Cabala, in Hebrew, is an occult religion or philosophy developed by certain rabbis based on mystical interpretations of scripture.

   D. Cabala is the secret artifices of machinations of people, of close design and not for popular consumption.

   E. Cabala is hidden knowledge and experience. Its doctrines are handed down orally through generations.

   F. From early Jewish history, Cabala was a traditional framework for laws, legends and ideas to become associated with the Pentateuch, the books of Moses: Genesis, Exodus, Leviticus, Numbers, and Deuteronomy.

   G. The word *cabinet,* such as the President's Cabinet, evolved from Cabala. It means deep discussion by a few.

2. CABALA HAS THREE ASPECTS

   A. The emanation (sephiroth) doctrine.

B. The methods for interpreting the Scriptures.

C. The Redeemer doctrine.

The Cabalists say all Scriptures have hidden meanings. For example, the phrase, "No fire on Sabbath," is interpreted: Fire is light, so turn on the light to be warm.

Cabala is strongly based upon the symbolism of numbers.

NOTE: (*Principalities and Powers,* by John Warwick Montgomery.)

3. THE ROSICRUCIAN ORDER ROSE UP OUT OF CABALA

A. Any inordinate desire for the supernatural always leads to occult infiltration.

B. Esoteric searchers for unknown information, or the secrets of divinity, and spirituality, can terminate in the occult.

C. Metaphysical concepts of human destiny can lead to the occult.

D. All deep mental concentrations must be God-directed or Satan will step in, intrude and misguide.

4. MYSTICISM NOTARIKON

Notarikon is an acoustic system. The initial or final letters of the words of a phrase might be joined to form a word, which is then given occult significance. The significance of another word might be explained by expanding it into a phrase, using each letter of the original words as the initial letters of one word of the phrase.

5. THE THEMURAH ("TRANSPORTATION")

A. Themurah consists of transposing the letters of a word, or more frequently, replacing them with artificial equivalents obtained from one or another of a group of formal anagrams. The most popular types of replacements are the following:

1) By folding the alphabet in the center and placing one-half below the other, we obtain a "code" in which corresponding letters on the upper and lower lines could be substituted for each other in interpreting a Scripture passage.

2) The lower line could be reversed and similar substitutions made.

B. We must know precisely to what use gematria, notarikon, and themurah were put. These methods were used for two prime purposes.

1) First and foremost, to derive from the Scriptures a hidden, occult meaning.

2) Secondly, to validate the Scriptures as literally inspired of God by showing the remarkable numerical relationships which presumably existed in them.

6. THE EMANATION (SEPHIROTH) DOCTRINE

The Cabalists conceived that God's attributes were actually emanations from Him. These emanations were beings, per se. They were produced by a voluntary retraction, or self-limitation of God. This retraction was considered the birth pain of creation. To the Cabalists, God was the infinite, the boundless, the limitless, the En or Ain Soph.

The lower the particular emanation, the more removed it was from God's sublimity and transcendence, and the less perfect it was. The entire ten emanations were repeated on four levels so that there were forty regressions from God to our world. A variant scheme limits the number of worlds to three; the worlds of angels, celestrial bodies, and elements. This is the presentation of this subject given by Menahem Recanati.

7. THREE PRIMARY CABALISTIC METHODS OF INTERPRETING THE BIBLE WERE EMPLOYED

Gematria, defined as "a process of creating equivalences from the numerical values of words." This method is used in the Hebrew, Latin and Greek languages, i.e. God is solely good and the first of all beings for Yahveh$i$ 1+5+6+5+=17; *tov* ("good") =9+6+2=17; *rishon* ("first")=2+1+3+6+5=17.

The Cabalic and the Talmudic teachers vied with each other in the Jewish circles, both of them attempting to discover a maximum amount of data and proof of the authenticity of the Scriptures.

The Cabala, in reaction to the Talmudic approach, emphasized the text itself (the letters, words, their numerical equivalents, etc.) instead of making attempts at allegorical interpretation and extension of the text to cover specific problems.

Cabalists were more interested in the letters of the text than were the Talmudists. They were certainly not literal interpreters of it.

The Karaites, another movement reacting against Talmudic casuistry, were the extreme literalists of the Jewish tradition. Their concern was limited to the surface meaning of the text. Karaites would light no fires on the Sabbath, even in the coldest climate, because the Torah states that fires should not be lit on that day. The Talmudists, in their characteristic way, asserted that it was alright to light fires the day before the Sabbath, and let them burn on the Sabbath.

The Cabalist, when interpreting the passage in question, would have worked the gematrias of the Hebrew words for "fire," "light" etc. And derived a "hidden" meaning from them. Just as the casuistry of the Talmudists drove the Cabalists to their right, the rationalistic and scholarly attitude of mind, which the Cabalists inherited from Alexandria and employed in formulating the sephiroth doctrine, would not permit them to be satisfied with the simple and unsophisticated approach of the Karaites.

The Cabala entered the Christian tradition through the work of one of the most remarkable figures of the Italian High Renaissance. Giovanni Pico della Mirandola lived only 31 years (1463-1494), but he typified in every way the ideal Renaissance man. All knowledge was his province, and esoteric knowledge in particular. He published no fewer than 900 theses on all manner of topics and was even willing to pay the travel expenses of those who wished to debate him. He wrote a major work against astrology in the same vein, claiming that men were free even of stellar and cosmic control.

8. WHAT IS THE SPIRITUAL VALUE OF CABALA?

How many Jews and Christians and esoteric searchers for truth have wandered in Cabalistic labyrinths? Can such wanderings be justified? If not, can historical understanding at least clarify the motivations involved?

The Truth-Value of the Emanation (Sephiroth) Doctrine.

This Cabalistic doctrine must be rejected on two counts. First, its truth is not sufficiently attested by Scriptural revelation, the only means by which such a metaphysical concept could in principle be verified. The Bible does not mention the sephiroth anywhere within it, and more importantly, the tenor of some passages of Scripture seems definitely to contradict such a notion.

A. I Timothy 2:5, *For there is one God, and one mediator between God and men, the man Christ Jesus.*

B. Colossians 2:18-19, *Let no man beguile you of your reward in a voluntary humility and worshipping of angels, intruding into those things which he hath not seen, vainly puffed up by his fleshly mind,*

v. 19, *And not holding the Head, from which all the body by joints and bands having nourishment ministered, and knit together, increaseth with the increase of God.*

C. II Peter 1:20, *Knowing this first, that no prophecy of the scripture is of any private interpretation.*

The Greek word for "private" can also be translated "secret."

NOTES

INDIANA CHRISTIAN UNIVERSITY

DEMONOLOGY & DELIVERANCE II
PRINCIPALITIES & POWERS

Lesson 14

DO THE STARS INFLUENCE HUMAN LIFE?

READING:

Genesis 1:14-19, *And God said, Let there be lights in the firmament of the heaven to divide the day from the night; and let them be for signs, and for seasons, and for days, and years:*

v. 15, *And let them be for lights in the firmament of the heaven to give light upon the earth: and it was so.*

v. 16, *And God made two great lights; the greater light to rule the day, the lesser light to rule the night: he made the stars also.*

v. 17, *And God set them in the firmament of the heaven to give light upon the earth,*

v. 18, *And to rule over the day and over the night, and to divide the light from the darkness: and God saw that it was good.*

v. 19, *And the evening and the morning were the fourth day.*

INTRODUCTION:

The greatest ascendancy of astrology since the fall of Babylon has come to our modern world. There is an obsession with astrology in this country. It is the new religion. It comes in new and old guises.

The word "astrology" comes from two Greek words:

    A. *Astra* meaning "star."

    B. *Logos* meaning "word, reason, or logic."

    Thus, astrology means, "the word from the stars."

    Many of God's people are ignorant of the beginnings of astrology and its hidden power.

Astronomy is a science of the celestial bodies.

Astrology claims to interpret the influence of the heavenly bodies on man, earth, and each other. Here the devil enters human affairs to speak and communicate lies. The zodiac is the tool and symbol of astrology.

1. WHAT IS ASTROLOGY?

A. Astrology is used as a personality decoder.

B. Millions of people will make no major decision before consulting the stars.

C. In the early history of mankind, when there was no electricity or any bright lights, man could witness the starry heavens in their glory every night. The positions of the stars and planets at different seasons of the year amazed men. Their shapes caused men to believe that the stars were imaginary figures like men and animals.

2. THE DIVINE PURPOSE OF THE STARS

A. God said the stars are for signs, seasons, days and years.

Genesis 1:14, *And God said, Let there be lights in the firmament of the heaven to divide the day from the night; and let them be for signs, and for seasons, and for days, and years.*

B. The function of stars is recorded.

Jeremiah 31:35-37, *Thus saith the LORD, which giveth the sun for a light by day, and the ordinances of the moon and of the stars for a light by night, which divideth the sea when the waves thereof roar; The LORD of hosts is his name:*

v. 36, *If those ordinances depart from before me, saith the LORD, then the seed of Israel also shall cease from being a nation before me for ever.*

v. 37, *Thus saith the LORD; If heaven above can be measured, and the foundations of the earth searched out beneath, I will also cast off all the seed of Israel for all that they have done, saith the LORD.*

3. HOW WAS ASTROLOGY BORN?

A. When mankind lost fellowship with the true God who had made him, he began worshipping many things, including the sun and stars.

Romans 1:25, *Who changed the truth of God into a lie, and worshipped and served the creature more than the Creator, who is blessed for ever. Amen.*

B. God was very careful with his people to warn them of star worship, lunar worship, and sun worship.

Deuteronomy 4:19, *And lest thou lift up thine eyes unto heaven, and when thou seest the sun, and the moon, and the stars, even all the host of heaven, shouldest be driven to worship them, and serve them, which the LORD thy God hath divided unto all nations under the whole heaven.*

C. Jehovah began the decalogue with the warning.

Exodus 20:3, *Thou shalt have no other gods before me.*

v. 4, *Thou shalt not make unto thee any graven image, or any likeness of any thing that is in heaven above, or that is in the earth beneath, or that is in the water under the earth:*

D. When a human worships beasts, trees, mountains, rocks, or stars, he opens his inner man to deception and demon possession.

I Corinthians 10:19-20, *What say I then? that the idol is any thing, or that which is offered in sacrifice to idols is any thing?*

v. 20, *But I say, that the things which the Gentiles sacrifice, they sacrifice to devils, and not to God: and I would not that ye should have fellowship with devils.*

E. Over 100 million Americans are devotees and adherents of astrology and another 40 million have fun playing with it.

F. In England, the *Sunday Times* stated that 2/3 of the population of Great Britain read horoscopes.

4. GOD SAID TO HIS PEOPLE ISRAEL, "BEWARE OF ASTROLOGY"

Deuteronomy 4:19, *And lest thou lift up thine eyes unto heaven, and when thou seest the sun, and the moon, and the stars, even all the host of heaven, shouldest be driven to worship them, and serve them, which the LORD thy God hath divided unto all nations under the whole heaven.*

This could also be read, "And *beware* lest you lift up your eyes..." It is a warning.

5. GOD ACCUSED ISRAEL OF SPIRITUAL ADULTERY BY ASTROLOGY

Deuteronomy 17:3, *And hath gone and served others gods, and worshipped them, either the sun, or moon, or any of the host of heaven, which I have not commanded.*

This could be also be read, "...which I have *forbidden*"

6. ISRAEL'S KINGS LEAD THE NATION DOWN

II Kings 21:3-5, *For he built up again the high places which Hezekiah his father had destroyed; and he reared up altars for Baal, and made a grove, as did Ahab king of Israel; and worshipped all the host of heaven, and served them.*

v. 4, *And he built altars in the house of the LORD, of which the LORD said, In Jerusalem will I put my name.*

v. 5, *And he built altars for all the host of heaven in the two courts of the house of the LORD.*

Manasseh was king of Jerusalem for 55 years. He led the nation into demon worship. Generation after generation were star-struck (luna-tic).

7. ASTROLOGY AND CONFUSION

Isaiah 47:13, *Thou art wearied in the multitude of thy counsels. Let now the astrologers, the stargazers, the monthly prognosticators, stand up, and save thee from these things that shall come upon thee.*

This was Babylonian captivity and Israel did not seek God to know how to live.

8. THE PROPHET JEREMIAH REBUKED THE BACKSLIDDEN PEOPLE OF ISRAEL

Jeremiah 8:2, *And they shall spread them before the sun, and the moon, and all the host of heaven, whom they have loved, and whom they have served, and after whom they have walked, and whom they have sought, and whom they have worshipped: they shall not be gathered, nor be buried; they shall be for dung upon the face of the earth.*

Another translation reads:

Jeremiah 8:2a, *And they will scatter the corpses before the sun, and the moon, and all the host of heaven, whom the dead have loved, and whom they have served, and after whom they have walked, and whom they have sought, inquired of and required, and whom they have worshipped.*

9. THE NIGHT THE EMPIRE DIED, THE ASTROLOGERS WERE SEEK-

ING THE STARS TO SHOW THEM WHAT TO DO

A. Daniel 2:2, *Then the king commanded to call the magicians, and the astrologers, and the sorcerers, and the Chaldeans, for to shew the king his dreams. So they came and stood before the king.*

B. Daniel 2:10, *The Chaldeans answered before the king, and said, There is not a man upon the earth that can shew the king's matter: therefore there is no king, lord, nor ruler, that asked such things at any magician, or astrologer, or Chaldean.*

C. Daniel 2:27, *Daniel answered in the presence of the king, and said, The secret which the king hath demanded cannot the wise men, the astrologers, the magicians, the soothsayers, shew unto the king.*

D. Daniel 4:7, *Then came in the magicians, the astrologers, the Chaldeans, and the soothsayers: and I told the dream before them; but they did not make known unto me the interpretation thereof.*

E. Daniel 5:7, *The king cried aloud to bring in the astrologers, the Chaldeans, and the soothsayers. And the king spake, and said to the wise men of Babylon, Whosoever shall read this writing, and shew me the interpretation thereof, shall be clothed with scarlet, and have a chain of gold about his neck, and shall be the third ruler in the kingdom.*

It was doomsday in Babylon. It was the last night of the empire. Babylon was facing the Medes and Persians.

The astrologers of Babylon answered,

Daniel 5:11, *There is a man in thy kingdom, in whom is the spirit of the holy gods; and in the days of thy father light and understanding and wisdom, like the wisdom of the gods, was found in him; whom the king Nebuchadnezzar thy father, the king, I say, thy father, made master of the magicians, astrologers, Chaldeans, and soothsayers.*

NOTES

INDIANA CHRISTIAN UNIVERSITY

DEMONOLOGY & DELIVERANCE II
PRINCIPALITIES & POWERS

Lesson 15

WHAT IS HYPNOSIS?

READING:

Isaiah 26:3, *Thou wilt keep him in perfect peace, whose mind is stayed on thee: because he trusteth in thee.*

INTRODUCTION:

Hypnosis is riding a high wave of popularity in this country. It is being used in a multiplicity of forms from entertainment to medicine.

1. WHAT IS HYPNOSIS:

Mary Lange, writer: "There's just one thing certain, nobody knows what it is or why it works."

   A. Some say it is an altered state of mind, or the function of the subconscious mind.

   B. It has been called "a scientific tool capable of penetrating the deepest crevices of the mind, a potent sedative and an aesthetic agent, a back-door entrance to the mind."

   C. In 1958, the American Medical Association accepted hypnosis as a therapeutic technique and today more than 5,000 physicians use hypnosis in their practices. No doubt it is being used to bring relief from many various ills.

   However, the Medical Association also warned that it should be used with caution lest it also produce very detrimental effects.

   D. Historically, hypnosis has its roots deep in mysticism and sorcery. Our generation must learn that it is not a magic wand or an instant panacea from all worries, fears, poor memories or objectionable personalities.

   The Lord Jesus exhorted that we should *love the Lord thy God with. . .all thy mind.* (Matthew 22:37). He is more powerful than any hypnotist. God's Word says: *Think on these things. . .* (Philippians 4:8).

2. HOW IS HYPNOTISM BEING USED IN AMERICA

A. The news media gives it great expression. Also there is much advertising in newspapers and magazines.

B. The obstetrician asks to hypnotize a mother to have her baby.

C. The dentist asks if you want hypnotism for dentistry.

D. Some dietitians claim they can help you lose weight by hypnotism.

E. Hypnosis has been used in court trials seeking truth.

F. Psychotherapists seek to remove fear by hypnosis.

G. Hypnosis has been used to stop smoking or drinking.

H. Every large city phone book lists hypnotists to "help" the troubled American. It has catchy phrases and bright advertisements.

I. The devil is out to capture the total human personality.

3. WHAT DOES IT FEEL LIKE TO BE HYPNOTIZED?

Dr. Sandra Stege Mims, Ph.D.: "Hypnosis is a very pleasant experience and the subject wants it to continue, so he allows it to work. It feels so good that the subject wants to prolong the feeling."

4. WHAT HAPPENS TO THE MIND AND BODY DURING HYPNOTISM?

The body is immobile. Sometimes it reacts to the hypnotist in movements. The mind goes into neutral and the willpower resistance is broken down. The human under hypnosis is supposed to divulge information as the mind understands it.

5. CAN ANY PERSON BE HYPNOTIZED?

No, you must submit your will and your mind to the hypnotist.

6. CAN HYPNOTISM BECOME A HABIT LIKE ALCOHOL OR NICOTINE?

Yes, you might receive relief from stress, fear, or oppression, but when the hurt returned, you would crave the same remedy. You can also be taught to hypnotize yourself.

7. **HOW CAN YOU BE HURT BY HYPNOTISM?**

   It can alter your mind. The doctors say it could weaken your willpower or your resisting power to be your OWN.

8. **HYPNOTIZED WITNESSES UNACCEPTABLE IN COURT.**

   A. A psychiatrist says, "Witnesses previously hypnotized by police should not be allowed to testify in court because their memories may have been altered by the people who hypnotized them."

   He says that witnesses hypnotized by police will come to believe the authority's version of events instead of remembering what really happened.

   B. Dr. Martin Orne, a professor of psychiatry at the University of Pennsylvania says, "If the hypnotist has certain beliefs, he will create memories in the subject's mind. Hypnosis makes recall less reliable, but provides more information that can be checked out." Dr. Orne also said he is frequently called upon by defense attorneys to knock down the testimony of witnesses who have been hypnotized by police.

   C. Sigmund Freud used hypnosis to get his patients to recall early childhood memories, but in his later writings he conceded that those recollections could not be checked for accuracy.

9. **HYPNOSIS MAKES STRANGE CLAIMS**

   A. Psychogenic impotence: Your mind is the most remarkable part of the human body. Your mind is a treasure; keep it, protect it with fences of truth and power.

   B. "Hypnotism can be a double aid to standard counseling for psychogenic impotence," declares Dr. Harold B. Crasilneck of the American Society of Clinical Hypnosis. "My own work," he said, "shows that the technique can help men recognize the emotional roots of their problems and also build their sexual confidence by demonstrating how much body control they are capable of."

   C. Hypnosis and exorcism: Dr. Richard P. Kluft says that hypnosis can bring unity to the patient who is torn by multiple personalities.

   D. With hypnotherapy, the personalities that give an "Eve" three faces, or another patient four names, can converse with each other and eventually integrate.

10. WHAT GOD SAYS ABOUT YOUR MIND

A. Let the Holy Spirit rule both your conscious and subliminal mind.

Isaiah 26:3, *Thou wilt keep him in perfect peace, whose mind is stayed on thee because he trusteth in thee.*

B. Don't dwell on negative things, but think on good things.

Philippians 4:8, *Finally, brethren, whatsoever things are true, whatsoever things are honest, whatsoever things are just, whatsoever things are pure, whatsoever things are lovely, whatsoever things are of good report; if there be any virtue, and if there be any praise, think on these things.*

C. Fill your mind with the Word of God.

Romans 12:2, *And be not conformed to this world: but be ye transformed by the renewing of your mind, that ye may prove what is that good, and acceptable, and perfect, will of God.*

Philippians 2:5, *Let this mind be in you, which was also in Christ Jesus.*

D. Cover your mind with the blood of Jesus. God's power can purify even your dreams.

II Corinthians 10:4-5, *(For the weapons of our warfare are not carnal, but mighty through God to the pulling down of strong holds;)*

v. 5, *Casting down imaginations, and every high thing that exalteth itself against the knowledge of God, and bringing into captivity every thought to the obedience of Christ.*

11. HOW TO PROTECT YOUR MIND

Here are seven things you can do to protect your mind:

1) Don't read pornographic literature. It not only remains in your conscious, but is stored in your subconscious mind.

2) Don't listen to hard rock music. It will bring a jungle spirit into your inner being. It came from the pagans of Africa. If you indulge in hard rock, all of its wildness will nest in your subconscious being.

3) Don't take dope. Drugs of all kinds open the door to your subconscious mind. It creates unreality which filters through to the conscious mind.

4) Don't drink alcohol. Alcohol can cause you to become drunk, render you senseless, and opens the doors to your subconscious mind, filling it with deceptions of hell.

5) Don't watch far-out programs on television, especially X-rated programming.

6) Don't go to adult movies and watch sensual, immoral, and dirty motion pictures.

7) Don't permit anyone to ever hypnotize you. Don't entrust your mind to any person on the face of this earth. Protect your mind from all sorts of ESP, seances, oriental meditations and hypnotism. God will not control your mind. . .the devil must not! You have the key. . .hold it!

NOTES

INDIANA CHRISTIAN UNIVERSITY

DEMONOLOGY & DELIVERANCE
PRINCIPALITIES & POWERS

Lesson 16

OF DEMONS AND DISEASE

READING:

John 10:10, *The thief cometh not, but for to steal, and to kill, and to destroy: I am come that they might have life, and that they might have it more abundantly.*

INTRODUCTION:

Are some diseases caused by evil spirits? The Bible has the best answer. Certainly not all diseases are demon related.

1. **SATAN BROUGHT SORES UPON JOB**

   Job 2:7, *So went Satan forth from the presence of the LORD, and smote Job with sore boils from the sole of his foot unto his crown.*

   Job 2:8, *And he took him a potsherd to scrape himself withal; and he sat down among the ashes.*

2. **EPILEPSY**

   A. Matthew 4:24, *And his fame went throughout all Syria: and they brought unto him all sick people that were taken with divers diseases and torments, and those which were possessed with devils, and those which were lunatic, and those that had the palsy; and he healed them.*

   B. Matthew 17:15-18, *Lord, have mercy on my son: for he is lunatic, and sore vexed: for ofttimes he falleth into the fire, and oft into the water.*

   v. 16, *And I brought him to thy disciples, and they could not cure him.*

   v. 17, *Then Jesus answered and said, O faithless and perverse generation, how long shall I be with you? how long shall I suffer you? bring him hither to me.*

   v. 18, *And Jesus rebuked the devil; and he departed out of him: and the child was cured from that very hour.*

C. Luke 9:37-43, *And it came to pass, that on the next day, when they were come down from the hill, much people met him.*

v. 38, *And, behold, a man of the company cried out, saying, Master, I beseech thee, look upon my son: for he is mine only child.*

v. 39, *And, lo, a spirit taketh him, and he suddenly crieth out; and it teareth him that he foameth again, and bruising him hardly departeth from him.*

v. 40, *And I besought thy disciples to cast him out; and they could not.*

v. 41, *And Jesus answering said, O faithless and perverse generation, how long shall I be with you, and suffer you? Bring thy son hither.*

v. 42, *And as he was yet a-coming, the devil threw him down, and tare him. And Jesus rebuked the unclean spirit, and healed the child, and delivered him again to his father.*

v. 43, *And they were all amazed at the mighty power of God. . .*

3. POSSESSION

A. Matthew 10:1, 8, *And when he had called unto him his twelve disciples, he gave them power against unclean spirits, to cast them out, and to heal all manner of sickness and all manner of disease.*

v. 8, *Heal the sick, cleanse the lepers, raise the dead, cast out devils: freely ye have received, freely give.*

B. Luke 8:26-39, *And they arrived at the country of the Gadarenes, which is over against Galilee.*

v. 27, *And when he went forth to land, there met him out of the city a certain man, which had devils long time, and ware no clothes, neither abode in any house, but in the tombs.*

v. 28, *When he saw Jesus, he cried out, and fell down before him, and with a loud voice said, What have I to do with thee, Jesus, thou Son of God most high? I beseech thee, torment me not.*

v. 29, *(For he had commanded the unclean spirit to come out of the man. For oftentimes it had caught him: and he was kept bound with chains and in fetters; and he brake the bands, and was driven of the devil into the wilderness.)*

v. 30, *And Jesus asked him, saying, What is thy name? And he said, Legion: because many devils were entered into him.*

v. 31, *And they besought him that he would not command them to go out into the deep.*

v. 32,   *And there was there an herd of many swine feeding on the mountain: and they besought him that he would suffer them to enter into them. And he suffered them.*

v. 33,   *Then went the devils out of the man, and entered into the swine: and the herd ran violently down a steep place into the lake, and were choked.*

v. 34,   *When they that fed them saw what was done, they fled, and went and told it in the city and in the country.*

v. 35,   *Then they went out to see what was done; and came to Jesus, and found the man, out of whom the devils were departed, sitting at the feet of Jesus, clothed, and in his right mind: and they were afraid.*

v. 36,   *They also which saw it told them by what means he that was possessed of the devils was healed.*

v. 37,   *Then the whole multitude of the country of the Gadarenes round about besought him to depart from them; for they were taken with great fear: and he went up into the ship, and returned back again.*

v. 38,   *Now the man out of whom the devils were departed besought him that he might be with him: but Jesus sent him away, saying,*

v. 39,   *Return to thine own house, and shew how great things God hath done unto thee. And he went his way, and published throughout the whole city how great things Jesus had done unto him.*

4.   THIS WOMAN WHOM SATAN HAS BOUND

Luke 13:16, *And ought not this woman, being a daughter of Abraham, whom Satan hath bound, lo, these eighteen years, be loosed from this bond on the sabbath day?*

5.   INSANITY

Mark 5:1-8, *And they came over unto the other side of the sea, into the country of the Gadarenes.*

v.2, *And when he was come out of the ship, immediately there met him out of the tombs a man with an unclean spirit,*

v. 3, *Who had his dwelling among the tombs; and no man could bind him, no, not with chains:*

v. 4, *Because that he had been often bound with fetters and chains, the chains had been plucked asunder by him, and the fetters broken in pieces: neither could any man tame him.*

v. 5, *And always, night and day, he was in the mountains, and in the tombs, crying, and cutting himself with stones.*

v. 6, *But when he saw Jesus afar off, he ran and worshipped him,*

v. 7, *And cried with a loud voice, and said, What have I to do with thee, Jesus, thou son of the most high God? I adjure thee by God, that thou torment me not.*

v. 8, *For he said unto him, Come out of the man, thou unclean spirit.*

6. OPPRESSION

Acts 10:38, *How God anointed Jesus of Nazareth with the Holy Ghost and with power: who went about doing good, and healing all that were oppressed of the devil; for God was with him.*

7. ISSUE OF BLOOD

Matthew 9:20, *And, behold, a woman, which was diseased with an issue of blood twelve years, came behind him, and touched the hem of his garment.*

8. DUMBNESS

A. Matthew 9:32, *As they went out, behold, they brought to him a dumb man possessed with a devil.*

v. 33, *And when the devil was cast out, the dumb spake: and the multitudes marvelled, saying, It was never so seen in Israel.*

B. Luke 11:14, *And he was casting out a devil, and it was dumb. And it came to pass, when the devil was gone out, the dumb spake; and the people wondered.*

9. BLINDNESS

Matthew 12:22, *Then was brought unto him one possessed with a devil, blind, and dumb: and he healed him, insomuch that the blind and dumb both spake and saw.*

10. UNCLEANNESS

Luke 4:33-36, *And in the synagogue there was a man, which had a spirit of an unclean devil, and cried out with a loud voice,*

v. 34, *Saying, Let us alone; what have we to do with thee, thou Jesus of Nazareth? art thou come to destroy us? I know thee who thou art; the Holy One of God.*

v. 35, *And Jesus rebuked him, saying, Hold thy peace, and come out of him. And when the devil had thrown him in the midst, he came out of him, and hurt him not.*

v. 36, *And they were all amazed, and spake among themselves, saying, What a word is this! for with authority and power he commandeth the unclean spirits, and they come out.*

11. SUICIDE

Matthew 27:5, *And he cast down the pieces of silver in the temple, and departed, and went and hanged himself.*

12. GRECIAN VEXATION—AN UNCLEAN SPIRIT

Mark 7:24-30, *And from thence he arose, and went into the borders of Tyre and Sidon, and entered into an house, and would have no man know it: but he could not be hid.*

v. 25, *For a certain woman, whose young daughter had an unclean spirit, heard of him, and came and fell at his feet;*

v. 26, *The woman was a Greek, a Syrophenician by nation; and she besought him that he would cast forth the devil out of her daughter.*

v. 27, *But Jesus said unto her, Let the children first be filled: for it is not meet to take the children's bread, and to cast it unto the dogs.*

v. 28, *And she answered and said unto him, Yes, Lord: yet the dogs under the table eat of the children's crumbs.*

v. 29, *And he said unto her, For this saying go thy way; the devil is gone out of thy daughter.*

v. 30, *And when she was come to her house, she found the devil gone out, and her daughter laid upon the bed.*

13. VEXED BY THE DEVIL

Matthew 15:22, *And, behold, a woman of Canaan came out of the same coasts, and cried unto him, saying, Have mercy on me, O Lord, thou son of David; my daughter is grievously vexed with a devil.*

14. DROPSY

Luke 14:2, *And, behold, there was a certain man before him which had the dropsy.*

15. IMPEDIMENT OF SPEECH

Mark 7:32, *And they bring unto him one that was deaf, and had an impediment in his speech; and they beseech him to put his hand upon him.*

INDIANA CHRISTIAN UNIVERSITY

DEMONOLOGY & DELIVERANCE II
PRINCIPALITIES & POWERS

Lesson 17

WHAT IS EXORCISM?

READING:

Mark 16:17, *And these signs shall follow them that believe; In my name shall they cast out devils; they shall speak with new tongues.*

INTRODUCTION:

This is a complete study on this most important subject.

1. **WHERE SHOULD DEMONS BE CAST OUT?**

    A. Not necessarily by "closet" or private sessions.

    B. In the New Testament, demons were cast out:

    1) In church meetings.

       Luke 13:16, *And ought not this woman being a daughter of Abraham, whom Satan hath bound, lo, these eighteen years, be loosed from this bond on the sabbath day?*

    2) On streets around groups.

       Matthew 17:15-18, *Lord, have mercy on my son: for he is lunatic, and sore vexed: for ofttimes he falleth into the fire, and oft into the water.*

       v. 16, *And I brought him to thy disciples, and they could not cure him.*

       v. 17, *Then Jesus answered and said, O faithless and perverse generation, how long shall I be with you? how long shall I suffer you? bring him hither to me.*

       v. 18, *And Jesus rebuked the devil; and he departed out of him: and the child was cured from that very hour.*

    There was never any attempt to hide or conceal what was going on.

2. WHO SHOULD CAST OUT DEVILS?

A. The Lord Jesus Christ said, *...them that believe...*(Mark 16:17).

    1) Disciples did.

    Matthew 10:8, *Heal the sick, cleanse the lepers, raise the dead, cast out devils: freely ye have received, freely give.*

    2) Paul did.

    Acts 16:18, *And this did she many days. But Paul, being grieved, turned and said to the spirit, I command thee in the name of Jesus Christ to come out of her. And he came out the same hour.*

    3) Every believer should become involved in casting out demon spirits.

    Mark 16:17, *And these signs shall follow them that believe; In my name shall they cast out devils; they shall speak with new tongues;*

B. The only hope in today's world against the awful tide of supernatural demon manifestation is for the church to rise up to set men free. A person must have a right relationship with God to cast out devils.

3. HOW TO CAST OUT EVIL SPIRITS

A. The Word of God is the sword of the Spirit.

Ephesians 6:17, *And take the helmet of salvation, and the sword of the Spirit, which is the word of God.*

B. Repeat the Word of God.

Mark 11:23, *For verily I say unto you, That whosoever shall say unto this mountain, Be thou removed, and be thou cast into the sea; and shall not doubt in his heart, but shall believe that those things which he saith shall come to pass; he shall have whatsoever he saith.*

To confess with our lips is very important to the word "believe" in this Scripture. "Believe" is used once, while the word "say" is used three times. Jesus said, *...he shall have whatsoever he saith.*

4. EVIL SPIRITS

A. The Bible speaks of many kinds of evil spirits.

    1) Blind spirits

    2) Deaf spirits

    3) Deceiving spirits

   4) Seducing spirits

   5) Jealous spirits

   6) Insane spirits

   7) Epileptic spirits

   8) Familiar spirits

B. Demons are a class of fallen spirit beings of which the Bible takes frequent notice. These are sometimes called:

   1) Evil spirits

   2) Demons

   3) Devils

C. Demons seek human habitation. All evidence points to the fact that they are disembodied spirits, or spirits without corporality. Their desire is for embodiment. They will possess man or beast. Their activities are in harmony with the objectives of Satan and that is to defile the plans of God.

5. SOME EVIL SPIRITS ARE IMPRISONED IN THE WATERS OF THE EUPHRATES

REVELATION 9:14, *Saying to the sixth angel which had the trumpet, Loose the four angels which are bound in the great river Euphrates.*

6. DEMONS HAVE NO RIGHT

Demons have no right to dwell in the individual who professes the name of Christ. However, if the person is disobedient, self-willed, and intent upon his own course, and permits his life to continue empty of the things of God, the demon then has a right to return and take possession of the person.

Luke 11:24-26, *When the unclean spirit is gone out of a man, he walketh through dry places, seeking rest; and finding none, he saith, I will return unto my house whence I came out.*

v. 25, *And when he cometh, he findeth it swept and garnished.*

v. 26, *Then goeth he, and taketh to him seven other spirits more wicked than himself; and they enter in, and dwell there: and the last state of that man is worse than the first.*

7. IN EXORCISM, WHAT MUST A PERSON KNOW?

A. Demons act like Satan, their master.

B. Demons vary in strength.

C. Demons have pride-filled natures.

D. Many demons can live in one person at the same time.

E. Demons are filthy.

F. Demons are not to be feared in Christ.

8. THERE ARE "RELIGIOUS" DEMONS

A. There are religious demons who apparently have special talents for luring people into false religions.

B. Demons give false revelations and teach unscriptural doctrines to persons who lack humility and are possessed with undue personal ambitions.

C. The Bible clearly declares that this will happen in the last days.

I Timothy 4:1, *Now the Spirit speaketh expressly, that in the latter times some shall depart from the faith, giving heed to seducing spirits, and doctrines of devils.*

9. JESUS CHRIST, THE GREATEST EXORCIST

A. Luke 7:21, *And in that same hour he cured many of their infirmities and plagues, and of evil spirits; and unto many that were blind he gave sight.*

B. Luke 8:26-33, *And they arrived at the country of the Gadarenes, which is over against Galilee.*

v. 27, *And when he went forth to land, there met him out of the city a certain man, which had devils long time, and ware no clothes, neither abode in any house, but in the tombs.*

v. 28, *When he saw Jesus, he cried out, and fell down before him, and with a loud voice said, What have I to do with thee, Jesus, thou Son of God most high? I beseech thee, torment me not.*

v. 29, *(For he commanded the unclean spirit to come out of the man. For oftentimes it had caught him: and he was kept bound with chains and in fetters; and he brake the bands, and was driven of the devil into the wilderness.)*

v. 30, *And Jesus asked him, saying, What is thy name? And he said, Legion: because many devils were entered into him.*

v. 31, *And they besought him that he would not command them to go out into the deep.*

v. 32, *And there was there an herd of many swine feeding on the mountain: and they besought him that he would suffer them to enter into them. And he suffered them.*

v. 33, *Then went the devils out of the man, and entered into the swine: and the herd ran violently down a steep place into the lake, and were choked.*

C. Luke 9:1, *Then he called his twelve disciples together, and gave them power and authority over all devils, and to cure diseases.*

D. Luke 9:37-42, *And it came to pass, that on the next day, when they were come down from the hill, much people met him.*

v. 38, *And, behold, a man of the company cried out, saying, Master, I beseech thee, look upon my son: for he is mine only child.*

v. 39, *And, lo, a spirit taketh him, and he suddenly crieth out; and it teareth him that he foameth again, and bruising him hardly departeth from him.*

v. 40, *And I besought thy disciples to cast him out; and they could not.*

v. 41, *And Jesus answering said, O faithless and perverse generation, how long shall I be with you, and suffer you? Bring thy son hither.*

v. 42, *And as he was yet a-coming, the devil threw him down, and tare him. And Jesus rebuked the unclean spirit, and healed the child, and delivered him again to his father.*

E. Luke 11:14, *And he was casting out a devil, and it was dumb. And it came to pass, when the devil was gone out, the dumb spake; and the people wondered.*

F. Luke 11:24, *When the unclean spirit is gone out of a man, he walketh through dry places, seeking rest; and finding none, he saith, I will return unto my house whence I came out.*

G. Acts 10:38, *How God anointed Jesus of Nazareth with the Holy Ghost and with power: who went about doing good, and healing all that were oppressed of the devil; for God was with him.*

NOTES

INDIANA CHRISTIAN UNIVERSTIY

DEMONOLOGY & DELIVERANCE II
PRINCIPALITIES & POWERS

Lesson 18

APOCALYPTIC TIMES

READING:

Daniel 12:2, *And many of them that sleep in the dust of the earth shall awake, some to everlasting life, and some to shame and everlasting contempt.*

INTRODUCTION:

These are apocalyptic times.

It is wonderful to be alive and to be a reporter for "The Heavenly Times."

The portentous events of this lesson deal with the termination of a century and also the culmination of a millennium. It further deals with the final phase of human history upon the face of this earth.

The next thirty-odd years will have more to do with Biblical interpretation of history than the last 4,000 years combined. This seems incredible, yet each day of the future will prove this to be true.

1. SEAL THAT BOOK

Astronomical in importance is the truth that the key prophecies of the ages have been sealed for centuries. This amazing prophecy was given by Daniel in chapter twelve of his book.

Daniel 12:1-4, *And at that time shall Michael stand up, the great prince which standeth for the children of thy people: and there shall be a time of trouble, such as never was since there was a nation even to that same time: and at that time thy people shall be delivered, every one that shall be found written in the book.*

v. 2, And many of them that sleep in the dust of the earth shall awake, some to everlasting life, and some to shame and everlasting contempt.

v. 3, *And they that be wise shall shine as the brightness of the firmament; and they that turn many to righteousness as the stars for ever and ever.*

v. 4, *But thou, O Daniel, shut up the words, and seal the book even to the time of the end: many shall run to and fro, and knowledge shall be increased.*

This is one of the most astounding prophecies of the entire Bible. It says that at the end of time the people of Israel will be in their own land as a people with their own flag, and at that time the entire world shall have trouble such as never was since there was a nation. This situation is upon the world at this very moment. God says unequivocally that He will deliver the people of Israel at that time.

A. The two resurrections of the endgame (verse 2).

There is the resurrection of the just, and the resurrection of the wicked dead. How amazing that a man 900 years before Christ, by the power of the Holy Spirit, could see the end of the world with such precision.

B. Daniel prophesies of soul winners (verse 3).

Daniel prophesies that soul winners will become the diadems of eternity and will shine like stars forever. Surely, this should challenge every believer to be a soul winner for Christ.

C. The book is closed and sealed (verse 4).

Here is the commandment for the book to be closed and sealed until the time of the end.

We are now living in the time of the opening and disclosure of the great prophecies of the Bible. In this present amazing hour of revelation, the apocalyptic key is unlocking door after door of the great prophecies spoken by the mighty seers, such as Isaiah, Jeremiah, Ezekiel, Daniel and Joel; in the New Testament, Jesus Christ, and the apostles Peter, Paul and John.

Wise men are grappling with these prophetical locks and keys day and night seeking to find the right combination to open the door to the resplendent revelations of the Most High.

2. MAN'S FANTASY FUTURE

A. The learned men of this world are not studying prophecy. They are dreaming of a fantasy future.

B. Since Adam and Eve lost their true dream world in the Garden of Eden, where they did not labor by the sweat of their brow, nor groan in bodily pain, man has sought to regain this Utopia.

C. Tremendous concerted effort was made just after the Flood when mankind endeavored to build a tower which would reach into heaven itself (Genesis 11). From that confused failure, man has constantly tried to build a dream world without God.

D. Also, in fulfillment of Daniel 12:4, God says, ...*the time of the end: many shall run to and fro...*

As you probably realize, the greatest business on the face of this earth today is tourism. It nets more than 8 billion dollars annually. Never in the history of mankind have people so fervishly run to and fro.

E. This same verse says, . . .*and knowledge shall be increased.* It is this breakthrough in knowledge that man is using to create his fantasy dream world of the future. It is man's last try to make a paradise of plenty and leisure on this earth. His deadline is 2,000 A.D.

F. Man hopes to achieve his "fantasy future" with the magic of push-button automation. He already has automobiles equipped with push buttons to shift the gears, to raise the windows, and move the seat back, forward and upward. There is even a button to push for greasing the car.

Man is trying to bring Edenic bliss to the home with push buttons and not with Christ. Man's home of the future will be heated by the rays of the sun. I have already personally seen this in operation. He will even raise and lower the windows with buttons. I have also seen this in operation.

G. The housewife will push a button and cook an entire meal. She can be out of the house shopping while it is being cooked. The housewife of tomorrow will be able to cook her food by heatwaves in packages and without the use of a stove. We are even promised that we can take a bath by supersonic waves not needing a bathtub.

H. Today you can pick up your telephone and talk long distance by dialing directly and looking at the person you are talking with on the telephone screen. This is soon to become common usage.

I. In man's fantasy future, he will travel thousands of miles per hour in supersonic aircraft costing 50 million dollars each. He will fly from New York to London in an hour or hour and a half.

J. In that modern world, families will no longer use automobiles to go shopping at the local super plaza, but from the roof of their homes will use helicopters to go to the supermarket. The supermarkets will seat you on a moving belt and you can ride past the merchandise, pick out what you desire, place it on another belt and an attendant will place it in your car or helicopter.

K. In education, schools of the future will teach mostly by television and many subjects will be projected into the homes of the students.

L. Man is truly thinking of an "Alice in Wonderland" future. God is about to speak and say as He did in Genesis 11:6-7, *And the LORD said, Behold, the people is one, and they have all one language; and this they begin to do: and now nothing will be restrained from them, which they have imagined to do.*

v. 7, *Go to, let us go down, and there confound their language, that they may not understand one another's speech.*

M. Surely, history will repeat itself because man seeks to build his paradise without God. Man's greatest problem in this world of fantasy is himself. In his world of tomorrow, man will not know what to do with his time. His life will become boring. It will lead to universal violence, unparalleled crime, global moral breakdown, millions of divorces and broken homes, and more insane asylums.

Every outstanding medical authority in the world today fears man's fantasy future, because of the multitudes of mental breakdowns. Rather than an Edenic paradise, man will end up producing a world of irresponsible degenerates. The nations will be full of immoral youth, diseased in mind and body, who are at the same time boasting of their engineering feats in traveling into outer space and creating a push-button civilization. The curse of man from the beginning in his obsession to build a heaven on this earth without the assistance of God.

3. THE FINAL COUNTDOWN

A. Beyond doubt, every thinking person realizes our world is in its final countdown. We are now entering the final phase of the world crisis which will close the 6,000 year period of man on this earth. Only the intervening hand of God can prevent nations from committing international suicide and blowing up the world.

B. God will again intervene. He will not send His Son to Bethlehem as a babe or to Calvary as a Lamb, but Christ is coming forth riding in magnificent splendor with crowns upon His head to rule the nations and bring peace to this troubled world.

Revelation 19:11-16, *And I saw heaven opened and behold a white horse; and he that sat upon him was called Faithful and True, and in righteousness he doth judge and make war.*

v. 12, *His eyes were as a flame of fire, and on his head were many crowns; and he had a name written, that no man knew, but he himself.*

v. 13, *And he was clothed with a vesture dipped in blood: and his name is called The Word of God.*

v. 14, *And the armies which were in heaven followed him upon white horses, clothed in fine linen, white and clean.*

v. 15, *And out of his mouth goeth a sharp sword, that with it he should smite the nations: and he shall rule them with a rod of iron: and he treadeth the winepress of the fierceness and wrath of Almighty God.*

v. 16, *And he hath on his vesture and on his thigh a name written, KING OF KINGS, AND LORD OF LORDS.*

4. ON TO 2,000 A.D.

A. We are now at the final one-third of the final century of man's activity on this earth. What is to prophetically take place during these next several years? It is most interesting that one-third of the entire Bible is prophecy or predicting the future. Many of these prophecies are yet to be fulfilled in the final century. We shall observe these fulfillments in the hours, days and years before us.

1) Daniel 2:40, *And the fourth kingdom shall be strong as iron: forasmuch as iron breaketh in pieces and subdueth all things: and as iron that breaketh all these, shall it break in pieces and bruise.*

2) Daniel 2:41, *And whereas thou sawest the feet and toes, part of potters' clay, and part of iron, the kingdom shall be divided; but there shall be in it of the strength of iron, forasmuch as thou sawest the iron mixed with miry clay.*

B. God's prophetical future illustrates that the iron man will prevail. He says that he breaketh in pieces and subdueth all things. Fierce world leaders are to emerge on the political stage, and finally the Antichrist, who will be the strongest military man of all history, with the most fierce facial expressions and convincing tongue the world has ever known. The common man will be ground to powder by the fierceness of the political leaders of the future.

C. Nations will be iron nations. I believe Russia is one of these. She will suppress others and depress her own people until God's Word is fulfilled in Ezekiel 37-39, when God will conclude His controversy with Russia and international Communism on the fabled battlefields of Megiddo. (These chapters are worth any man's reading.)

D. Further, an iron man will successfully mold a United States of Europe with strong antagonistic boastings. It will be the resurrection of the ancient Roman Empire raised up to finally fulfill its destiny in its last-day anger against the true God.

6. THE CLAY MAN

A. Yet in the midst of this austere iron man's world, there will be existing this clay man's world whose chief aim in life will be pushbuttons, idleness, luxury and sin. While one part of the world prepares for death and destruction, the other part will be willing to pay for peace at any cost.

B. The clay man's world is very much in evidence today. Much of our world at this moment is led by the weak. This is true in the United Nations where the overwhelming voting power is among the Afro-Asian nations who are the emerging nations and do not possess able governments.

This is also seen in the financial world where credit is king and hard cash is seldom seen.

C. This can also be observed in the labor world where men, who do not understand what makes a business successful, dominate the policies of big business.

This is further seen in the educational world in great student uprisings with undisciplined youth, marching through the streets challenging their own governments, when in most cases they do not know the true issues at stake.

D. This is the world of mud which can be pushed over by the whims of the iron man. At this moment, dictatorship is only waiting for its most advantageous moment to sweep the clay man into the sea.

E. What are some of the sign posts for Christians to observe during these fatal days of the final one-third of the final century?

1) Cosmic Convulsions—From now until the time of the end, no one will be able to predict weather patterns, or know the causes of earthquakes, or know why floods will come and why droughts will follow the floods. Men will seek to build buildings which will turn back hurricanes and typhoons. He will seek to build reservoirs to hold flood waters and stop droughts. He will seek to create chemicals which will destroy all pestilences.

2) Famines—God's Word says that in the immediate future there will be tremendous famines on the face of the earth. This will probably be caused by unpredicted floods and droughts and the natural follower is unparalleled epidemics of diseases.

   In Matthew 24:8, Jesus told us that this will be the beginning of sorrows or the beginning of the great tribulation. From that time, man's push-button prosperity and wealth will be snapped and destroyed. In Luke 21:22, the Lord Jesus said, *For these be the days of vengeance, that all things which are written may be fulfilled.* This means the days ahead of us are prophetic days.

3) Children shall rise up against their parents—In our domestic world, prophetic wheels are grinding. In Mark 13:12, Jesus predicted, *Now the brother shall betray the brother to death, and the father the son; and the children shall rise up against their parents, and shall cause them to be put to death.*

   When a generation does not love its own parents, that generation is doomed. Paul said in II Timothy 3:1-2, *This know also, that in the last days perilous times shall come. For men shall be lovers of their own selves, covetous, boasters, proud, blasphemers, disobedient to parents, unthankful, unholy.*

   We live in a world today where parents cannot control their own children. There is a spirit of anarchy that prevails in youthful hearts today. This is because parents do not know God and do not train their children to first respect God, and secondly to respect law and order. There is an uncontrollable spirit prompting the youth of the world to rise up and revolt against society. This is one of the signs of the end.

7. THE BILLIONAIRES' CLUB

A. Though the world is in such domestic trouble, the giant commercial combines become stronger and stronger. There are now 69 billionaire companies on the New York Stock Exchange. This has risen from 25 in the last 15 years.

This hour of heaped-up treasure is described in James 5:1-7. He cries that the rich man will weep and howl for his miseries. There has never been in the history of the world such enmity between the "haves" and the "have nots."

B. In the religious world, we have several important factors:

1) We have the return of Israel to her own land, getting ready to receive her own Messiah.

In Matthew 24:32, Christ prophesied that when you see the fig tree blossom forth, you will know that summer is nigh. The world now sees the fig tree in full bloom.

2) Among church members, Jesus predicted in Matthew 24:12 that the love of many will wax cold. This means those that used to sing with great fervor, those that used to pray with great victory, have now joined the push-button age and the fantasy future of materialism. Paul further stated this in II Thessalonians 2:3. He said that there will be a "falling away" first. This resembles a military line where the enemy pours his shots into the line and many fall, only a few stand.

The devil is fighting to cause many to fall away from the fold. Jesus further gave a religious sign of the end in Matthew 24:5, 11, 23, 24. He said there will be false christs who will come and deceive many. There will be miracle workers and false dreamers who will provoke the people to join a world church for security reasons. They will finally join with the Antichrist against the true Christ.

8. NO PEACE

It is very significant that God's Word says that peace will be taken from the earth. From midsummer of 1914, when the first rifle shot signaled the beginning of World War I, this world has not known peace for even one day. For over one-half of a century civilization has traveled the road to Armageddon. It is traveling the last mile of that bloody road.

BIBLIOGRAPHY

Angels of Light? Hobart Freeman, (Plainfield: Logos, 1969).

Astrology, Occultism, and the Drug Culture Lambert T. Dolphin, Jr.,
   (Westchester: Good News Publishers, 1970).

Astrology, The Ancient Conspiracy Ben Adam,
   (Minneapolis: Dimension Books, 1963).

Bitten by Devils Dr. Lester Sumrall,
   (South Bend: World Harvest Press, 1966).

The Challenging Counterfeit Raphael Gasson,
   (Plainfield: Logos, 1966).

Charismatic Studies—Demon Power Dr. Lester Sumrall,
   (South Bend: Lester Sumrall Evangelistic Association, 1981).

Demons in the World Today Merrill F. Unger,
   (Wheaton: Tyndale House, 1980).

Demons The Answer Book Dr. Lester Sumrall,
   (Thomas Nelson Publishers, 1979).

Heavenly Deception Chris Elkins,
   (Wheaton: Tyndale House, 1980).

Hypnotism—Divine or Demonic Dr. Lester Sumrall,
   (South Bend: Lester Sumrall Evangelistic Association, No date listed).

Jesus Taught Me to Cast Out Devils Norvel Hayes,
   (Manna Christian Outreach, 1975).

A Modern Study of Demon Power—Questions and Answers
   Three book series by Dr. Lester Sumrall,
   (South Bend: Lester Sumrall Evangelistic Association, No date listed).

Placebo Howard Pittman,
   (Foxworth: Howard Pittman, 1981).

The Satan, Demons and Demon Possession Series (3 volumes) Kenneth Hagin,
   (Faith Library Publications, 1980).

Satan is Alive & Well On Planet Earth Hal Lindsey,
   (Grand Rapids: Zondervan Corporation, 1970).

Satan On The Loose Nicky Cruz,
        (Old Tappan: Fleming H. Revell, 1974).

Satan Seller Mike Warnkey
        (South Plainfield, N.J.: Bridge Publishing, Inc., 1972).

Satan and the Occult Charles R. Swindoll,
        (Fullerton: Insight For Living, 1972).

Seven Steps Toward Demon Possession Dr. Lester Sumrall,
        (South Bend: Lester Sumrall Evangelistic Association. No date listed).

Superstition Dr. Lester Sumrall,
        (South Bend: World Harvest Press, 1968).

The Three Habitations of Devils Dr. Lester Sumrall,
        (South Bend: World Harvest Press, 1965).

Unprovoked Murder—Insanity or Demon Possession? Dr. Lester Sumrall,
        (Tulsa: Harrison House, 1981).

War On the Saints Jesse Pen-Lewis,
        (London: Marshall Brothers, 1912).

The Weird World of the Occult Walker Knight,
        (Wheaton: Tyndale house, 1972).

Witchcraft and Familiar Spirits Hilton Sutton,
        (Tulsa: Harrison House, 1982).

All of these books are available in the Christian Center Bookstore.

Bringing Quality Education To Your Home

In the last several years, educators around the country, including all of us here at Indiana Christian University, have seen a definite new trend in education. More and more, education is becoming decentralized and less campus-focused. This trend seems to be true in all areas of education, and especially in college work.

We here at ICU are very thankful that God has allowed us to be more than trend observers; we have been trendsetters. Because of his vision, insight and forethought--or should we say "prophetic knowledge"--Dr. Lester Sumrall developed a Bible curriculum which we can offer to the world through audio correspondence studies and video extension campuses. Due to his continuous travels as an evangelist and missionary during the years that he was trying to obtain his college education, Dr. Sumrall became acutely aware of the fact that traditional campus-based education would prove increasingly impractical for a greater number of people as their lives became more and more mobile. With this keen insight, Dr. Sumrall worked tirelessly to produce a college system that could go with the student rather than demanding that the student abandon his mission for a period of years to be anchored to a desk. The result was an off-campus program that makes Indiana Christian University literally a school with a global campus.

This correspondence program has allowed us to provide degree programs to ministers who cannot leave their churches, housewives who must stay with their families, missionaries in isolated mission posts, inmates in correctional institutions, patients in long-term medical facilities--and the list goes on and on.

In breaking beyond the limitation of our walls, ICU has begun to fulfill not only Dr. Sumrall's mandate, but also the directive left to us by Jesus Christ Himself: "Go ye therefore, and teach all nations..." (Matthew 28:19).

Introducing Indiana Christian University

Indiana Christian University is an independent school of higher learning serving all religious denominations. The student body and faculty reflect various types of church backgrounds, rather than any one denomination. The university is incorporated in the state of Indiana and grants degrees to those who satisfactorily complete the prescribed course of study.

The school's history dates to 1907, when a group of Christian people formed an institution for teaching the Bible and Bible-related subjects. It was chartered in the state of Indiana in 1923 as Indiana Bible Institute, becoming Indiana Bible College in 1934. The present name was adopted in 1940.

In addition to training ministers and professional people, the school has helped thousands of Christian laypeople gain a greater understanding of the Bible and has prepared them for Christian life. ICU became part of the Lester Sumrall Evangelistic Association in 1988. In 1990, the school was relocate from Indianapolis to its present home in South Bend. A merger with the former World Harvest Bib College was finalized in 1993, resulting in two campuses: Indianapolis and South Bend.

Programs of Study

A Certificate of Achievement in Charismatic Studies is awarded to students who successfully con plete the basic curriculum of charismatic studies with a grade average of 2.00 (C) or better. The bas curriculum includes: Faith, English, Christian Foundations, The Total Man, Human Illness and Divir Healing, Demon Power, The Gifts of the Holy Spirit, Prayer, and four hours of Practicum.

The Associate of Arts in Christian Ministry and Bachelor of Arts in Christian Ministry are awarded students who:

1. Demonstrate a Christian character which the school can recommend.
2. Complete the prescribed course (56 credit hours for the Associate of Arts in Christian Minist program; 112 credit hours for the Bachelor of Arts in Christian Ministry program) with a grad average of 2.00 (C) or better.

	Associate of Arts in Christian Ministry	Bachelor of Arts in Christian Ministry
Language Department		
English	3 hrs.	3 hrs.
Bible Department		
Old Testament	6 hrs.	16 hrs.
New Testament	6 hrs.	16 hrs.
Theology Department-must include the courses listed for the certificate program	21 hrs.	21 hrs.
Ministry Department		
Practicum	8 hrs.	16 hrs.
History Department	3 hrs.	6 hrs.
Electives	9 hrs.	34 hrs.

Earn College Credit
For This Course Through

1. Complete the application process.

   a) Complete and mail the application form along with the $25 application fee.

   b) Request your high school and/or college(s) to mail transcripts to ICU.

   c) Give the Pastor's Reference Form to your pastor and request that it be returned directly to ICU.

   d) In order to request consideration for life experience for practicum credits, submit a full resume showing dates of ministry and full responsibilities involved. Verification from an overseer or other recognizable authority must accompany each ministry assignment.

2. Upon acceptance you will receive:

   a) a transcript indicating any coursework which has been transferred from previous institutions, or life experience.

   b) a study plan indicating the ICU courses recommended to complete the program of study you are enrolling into. Be sure to keep this guideline and follow it carefully.

   c) a registration form for registering for your courses.

   d) a Sumrall Publications catalog for ordering your class study materials and tapes.

   e) a "How to Write a Term Paper" manual.

3. Complete the registration form and return it along with the appropriate fee to ICU.

4. Complete the order form for your class study materials and tapes and return it along with the proper payment to Sumrall Publishing.

5. When your class study materials and tapes arrive, read the lessons and listen to the tapes in the way most helpful to you. It is suggested that you read the lesson once, listen to the tape, and then read the lesson again. Complete the test which will be mailed to you upon the submission of your class registration. Carefully following the instructions in the term paper manual, write and submit a term paper on a topic related to the course. The paper should be 10-12 double-spaced, typewritten pages. Font size should not exceed 14 points and margins should not exceed 1 1/2 inches. All information from source material must be properly footnoted and listed in a bibliography.

For more information or application forms call 1-800-621-8885,
or write ICU PO Box 12, So. Bend, IN 46624 or email us at ICU@lesea.com